CULTURE SMART!
NIGERIA

Diane Lemieux

·K·U·P·E·R·A·R·D·

This book is available for special discounts for bulk purchases for sales promotions or premiums. Special editions, including personalized covers, excerpts of existing books, and corporate imprints, can be created in large quantities for special needs.

For more information in the USA write to Special Markets/Premium Sales, 1745 Broadway, MD 6–2, New York, NY 10019, or e-mail specialmarkets@randomhouse.com.

In the United Kingdom contact Kuperard publishers at the address below.

ISBN 978 1 85733 629 0
This book is also available as an e-book: eISBN 978 1 85733 630 6
British Library Cataloguing in Publication Data
A CIP catalogue entry for this book is available from the British Library

First published in Great Britain 2012
by Kuperard, an imprint of Bravo Ltd
59 Hutton Grove, London N12 8DS
Tel: +44 (0) 20 8446 2440   Fax: +44 (0) 20 8446 2441
www.culturesmart.co.uk
Inquiries: sales@kuperard.co.uk

Distributed in the United States and Canada
by Random House Distribution Services
1745 Broadway, New York, NY 10019
Tel: +1 (212) 572-2844   Fax: +1 (212) 572-4961
Inquiries: csorders@randomhouse.com

Series Editor Geoffrey Chesler
Design Bobby Birchall

Printed in Malaysia

About the Author

DIANE LEMIEUX is a Canadian-Dutch writer and journalist currently based in Lagos. Born in Quebec into a diplomatic family, she has lived and worked in eight countries around the world. She has a BA in Communication from the University of Ottawa in Canada, an MA in Development Studies from Leeds University in the United Kingdom, a postgraduate degree in International Relations from Amsterdam University in the Netherlands, and a diploma in Journalism from Bath University in the UK. She has written several books and articles on topics in the fields of intercultural communication, national diversity, and expatriate issues, and now specializes in Nigerian cultural life.

The Culture Smart! series is continuing to expand.
For further information and latest titles visit
www.culturesmart.co.uk

The publishers would like to thank **CultureSmart!**Consulting for its help in researching and developing the concept for this series.

CultureSmart!Consulting creates tailor-made seminars and consultancy programs to meet a wide range of corporate, public-sector, and individual needs. Whether delivering courses on multicultural team building in the USA, preparing Chinese engineers for a posting in Europe, training call-center staff in India, or raising the awareness of police forces to the needs of diverse ethnic communities, it provides essential, practical, and powerful skills worldwide to an increasingly international workforce.

For details, visit www.culturesmartconsulting.com

CultureSmart!Consulting and **CultureSmart!** guides have both contributed to and featured regularly in the weekly travel program "Fast Track" on BBC World TV.

contents

contents

Map of Nigeria

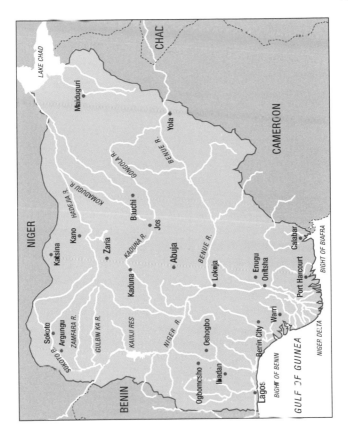

introduction

Nigeria is not, yet, a tourist destination. The potential is there. A large country, it has everything from sandy beaches and lush tropical jungles to fertile plains, beautiful mountains, and arid desert—but there is little tourism infrastructure. Most foreigners who visit the country do so purely for reasons of employment. Indeed, Nigerians themselves tend to travel within the country only for business reasons or to visit family. Few people take the time to appreciate the most exceptional aspect of Africa's most populous country: the vibrancy and cultural sophistication of its people.

The sheer cultural variety to be found within Nigeria is impressive, with around two hundred and fifty distinct ethno-linguistic groups. That said, three large groups dominate the cultural and political scene. The culture of the mainly Muslim Hausa-Fulani in the north is rooted in the once opulent city-states of the famed trans-Saharan trade routes. The Yoruba culture of the southwest has given rise to some of Africa's best-known art forms and has influenced religions and traditions in many countries through the out-migration of its people during the slave trade. Finally, the Igbo of the southeast have decentralized, republican traditions that have produced a culture of talented traders and businesspeople.

Competition for scarce resources during Nigeria's short history as an independent nation has fostered ingenuity and perseverance on the part of its ambitious citizens. They are natural entrepreneurs, and intelligent and shrewd negotiators. They are also proud. Acutely aware that they have been considered second-class people by Westerners for more than two hundred years, they are deeply aggrieved by their country's reputation for violence and corruption. Most are devout, gregarious, hardworking, and intensely critical of the culture of patronage and self-enrichment that grips much of the public sector.

Those who come to Nigeria to explore its economic potential cannot hope to be successful without the assistance of their Nigerian counterparts. Nigerians are not easy to get to know, however; their daily lives are extremely busy, with arduous commutes, long work hours, and many religious and family responsibilities. Furthermore, they are extremely sensitive to condescension—but to those who show a genuine desire to understand their culture, they offer warm hospitality and steadfast cooperation.

This book provides a snapshot of Nigeria today, a brief introduction to the ancient and complex systems of behavior, values, and attitudes that underlie the country's vibrant social and business life. It also opens the door to a fascinating culture that will undoubtedly play an increasingly important role in global affairs.

culture smart! nigeria

Key Facts

Official Name	Federal Republic of Nigeria	Member of the OAU, OPEC, and the Commonwealth
Capital City	Abuja	
Main Cities and Towns	Lagos, Kano, Calabar, Katsina, Port Harcourt, Enugu, Kaduna, Warri, Ibadan, Benin City, Jos, Zaria, Maiduguri, Bauchi	
Area	356,669 sq. miles (923,768 sq. km)	Divided into 36 states and 1 Federal Capital Territory
Terrain	Desert plains in the north, hills and plateaus in the middle belt, and tropical forests and a large delta basin in the south, along the coast	
Climate	Varies from arid in the north to tropical in the center and equatorial in the south	
Currency	Naira (N), divided into 100 kobo	USD1 = N117 GBP1 = N240 EUR1 = N220 (2011 est.)
Population	150 million (est.)	Africa's most populous country
Ethnic Makeup	There are more than 250 ethnic groups. The most populous and politically influential are Hausa and Fulani (29%), Yoruba (21%), Igbo (18%), Ijaw (10%), Kanuri (4%), Ibibio (3.5%), and Tiv (2.5%).	

National Languages	There are more than 500 languages; the most common are English (official), Hausa, Yoruba, Igbo, Fulani, and Pidgin.	
Religions	Sunni Muslim (50%), Christian (40%), indigenous beliefs (10%)	
Government	Federal republic; consecutive democratic elections since 1999	President is both chief of state and head of the government, elected for no more than two four-year terms. The three tiers of government are federal, state, and local.
Media	Private and state cable television networks available; DSTV is the main satellite TV provider. Many public and private radio stations in English and local languages	A variety of national and local newspapers are available, including *Guardian News*, *Business Day*, and *234 Next* (all also available online).
Electricity	220 volts, 50 Hz	3-flat-prong plugs. Adaptors required for US appliances; surge protectors and UPS battery packs advised.
Video/TV	PAL	
Internet Domain	.ng	
Telephone	Country code: 234	Several cell phone providers give good coverage.
Time Zone	GMT +1 throughout the year	

chapter one

LAND & PEOPLE

GEOGRAPHY

Nigeria is located in the elbow of western Africa, just before the coast shoots south. It is a large country—nearly one and a half times the size of the state of Texas or the country of France. Its southern border is the Atlantic Ocean; to the west is Benin, and to the east is Cameroon. In the north it shares a border with the Republic of Niger, and in the northeastern corner is Lake Chad.

Nigeria's territory—roughly 700 miles (1,125 km) wide and 650 miles (1,045 km) long—contains a rich and diverse geography. Along the coast the tropical forests and agricultural lands of the west gradually change to the lush mangrove swamps of the Niger Delta in the east. The middle belt is dominated by hills and plateaus, and mountains in the east. In the north, dry savanna gradually gives way to the Sahel desert area.

The country is effectively divided into three by the Niger and Benue rivers, which create a "Y" slightly south of the territory's center. The Niger enters the country in the northwest and flows southeast; the Benue flows in from the east. The two meet south of the capital, Abuja, and flow south to the Niger Delta and into the Atlantic.

The territory contains many natural resources. Petroleum reserves and natural gas are its most plentiful resource, found both offshore and in the Niger Delta. In terms of minerals, Nigeria has coal, iron, tin, columbite, lead, copper, and zinc, most of these located in the hills of the middle belt. Agricultural lands are most abundant in the middle belt and the north; fishing and forestry are prevalent along the southern coast.

Climate

Nigeria's climate is hot and tropical all year round, ranging from around 71°F to 97°F (22°C to 36°C). The main variable in climate is the amount and frequency of rain. The coast has an equatorial monsoonal climate with little variation in seasonal temperatures, high humidity, and the highest amount of rainfall. The central region has a tropical humid climate, while the north is dryer and has the least rainfall. Throughout the country there are two seasons: the dry and the rainy. The duration and strength of the rains decrease as you go north. On the coast, the rains begin in

February and peter off by August or September. In the northern regions, the rains fall from June or July to August. These regions also experience the largest range in temperatures: from around 110°F (43°C) in the dry months to the low 70s Fahrenheit (low 20s Celsius) during the rains.

From September to November, most of the country experiences clear skies, moderate temperatures, and lower humidity. From December through February, strong, dry northeasterly winds known as the harmattan blow fine dust from the Sahara into a dense fog that coats windows and cars with sand. While the harmattan reduces the humidity, this period is also known as flu season, during which there are increased incidents of allergies and respiratory and eye irritations.

THE PEOPLE

Nigeria is Africa's most populous country. Its

estimated population of about 150 million people is made up of more than two hundred and fifty different ethno-linguistic groups, each with its own history, culture, traditions, language, and identity. The three largest groups are: in the north, the Hausa-Fulani, who account for 29 percent of the population; in the southwest, the Yoruba, who account for roughly 21 percent; and in the southeast, the Igbo (pronounced "ee-boh"), who account for around 19 percent.

Other large groups include the Fulani, a pastoral people of the northern savannas; the Ijaw of the Niger Delta region; the Kanuri of the Lake Chad region; the Ibibio in the southeast, around the major city of Calabar; and the Nupe and Tiv of the middle-belt region.

There is also a large immigrant community, particularly from neighboring West African countries, as well as an important Syrian and Lebanese community that has been established for generations. Among the newer immigrant groups are significant numbers of East Indians, Chinese, and white Zimbabweans and South Africans.

Nigerians often find themselves hard-pressed to describe exactly what it is to be Nigerian: given the fact that the country was artificially created only a little more than seventy years ago, the concept of being Nigerian is relatively new. Furthermore, there is a significant difference in the cultural experiences of rural Nigerians (approximately 52 percent of the population), those of the lower and middle classes who work in the cities, and Nigeria's small wealthy elite, many of whom have lived and been educated abroad.

Language

It is estimated that there are five hundred and ten living languages in Nigeria, most of which fall within three major families: the Niger-Congo languages of the south, which include Yoruba and Igbo (both tonal languages); Hausa in the north, a Chadic group within the Afro-Asiatic family; and Kanuri, spoken in the northeast. English has been the official language of the country since independence in 1960 and is used in education, for business transactions, and in government. It is not spoken at all in some rural areas, however.

During the nineteenth century, Christian missionaries put indigenous languages such as Yoruba and Igbo into writing for the first time. They also developed the first written dictionaries in these languages and translated the Bible into local languages. In the 1930s the British colonial administration introduced a Latin-based alphabet called *boko* for the writing of Hausa. Hausa is itself a regional language as it is spoken in northern Nigeria and Niger, and in regions of Benin, Burkina Faso, Cameroon, the Central African Republic, Chad, Congo, Eritrea, Ghana, Sudan, and Togo.

Most Nigerians are multilingual. They speak at least one native language (but most often they will know more than one) and English, as well as Pidgin (a combination of indigenous languages and English that is recognized as a separate language).

Religion

Around 50 percent of the population are Sunni Muslim. Most northerners, and approximately one-third of the Yoruba in the southwest, are Muslims. Christians make up roughly 40 percent of the population, mostly in the south and middle belt. Protestantism and the evangelical churches are strongest in the southwest, while the peoples of the southeast are predominantly Catholic. The remaining 10 percent of the population continue to practice indigenous beliefs that are basically monotheist—they believe there is one God who exists in the spiritual world and who created all things. The link between man and God is provided by the divinities and spirits, who are worshipped through elaborate rituals.

DIVINERS

Even today, diviners are consulted to determine the causes of both good and bad luck, including the nature or cause of disease. Traditional healers continue to play an important role in health care delivery; the majority of the population depends on them for most ailments. Healers use primarily herbal remedies to treat patients holistically in terms of their physical, spiritual, mental, and material well-being.

The Constitution of Nigeria formally separates religion from matters of the state, but since independence (and particularly since the return to democracy in 1999) there has been an increasing politicization of religion; religious leaders have become spokespeople on behalf of their followers in petitioning the government for resources. Furthermore, particularly in the middle belt of the country where communities of Muslims and Christians live in close proximity, religion has become mixed up in local power politics.

A BRIEF HISTORY

The history of modern Nigeria dates back to October 1, 1960, the date of its official independence from British rule. The history of the people currently regrouped within its borders goes back much farther. There is evidence of habitation as far back as 9000 BCE. During the first millennium CE, permanent agricultural and livestock-rearing settlements evolved.

The societies within the area of present-day Nigeria displayed a diversity of governing structures. In the south and eastern middle-belt regions of the country, decentralized community-based structures predominated until colonization. Politically these were organized along an age-based hierarchy, led by the elders of patrilineal lines. Villages were linked through a market, where trade and intercommunity matters were settled. Ethnic groups such as the Igbo, the Ibibio, and the Tiv were linked through a common language and religious beliefs, while trade connected them to the wider West African community.

In the southwest, powerful centralized empires developed. By the twelfth century, the city-state of Ife-Ife (commonly known as just Ife and pronounced "ee-fay") was a regional power and the ancestral birthplace of the Yoruba people. It was a major trading center and is famous today for its elaborate bronze sculptures. The power of the Ife king (or *ooni*) lay not in military power (the kingdom never had a standing army) but in his divine connection to the spiritual world.

In the 1400s, in the kingdom of Benin, the town's administration was run by local hereditary chiefs allied to Benin's king. The palace administration, on the other hand, was run by a small group of individuals whose positions were obtained through a system of meritocracy. Benin expanded into an empire through a series of wars, extending

its lines of trade and influence late into the second millennium. From the fourteenth to the sixteenth centuries several strong, centralized city-states arose in the north of what is now Nigeria, including Katsina, Zaria, Kano, and Gobir. These developed from their position in the shifting

routes of trans-Saharan trade. Each state was
independent politically, though they were united
by a common Hausa language and the religion of
Islam. Each was headed by a king (or emir), was
managed through a large bureaucracy, and relied
on agriculture and livestock for trade. Gold,
slaves, and goods such as leather and leather
products, weapons, horses, and textiles were the
main commodities traded.

Islam in the North
Islam was first brought into the northern region
in the late eleventh century by traders,
missionaries, and the nomadic, pastoralist Fulani.
The first Hausa ruler to convert to Islam was Yaji
of Kano in 1370. For centuries, Islam coexisted
with indigenous beliefs and practices. Then, in
1804, a Fulani cleric, Usman dan Fodio, declared
a jihad against the corruption and un-Islamic
practices of the ruling Hausa elite. By 1810 the
Hausa states were united under the Sokoto
Caliphate, a grouping of decentralized emirates
all giving allegiance to dan Fodio, the first Caliph.

Thus, by the mid-nineteenth century, Islam
had spread throughout the northern territories
and was practiced exclusively by rural people and
city dwellers alike. The creation of the Caliphate
also ended the hundreds of years of interstate
wars in the north and dramatically improved the
economy and living conditions of the majority
of the region's people. Culturally, it united the
peoples of the north, creating a Muslim identity
that had never existed before.

The Spread of Christianity

Christianity was introduced on the coast by
Portuguese traders in the fifteenth century, but
it is only from the 1840s that it started to spread
throughout the country. Many Nigerian rulers
began to see the new religion as giving them a
spiritual and economic advantage over their
rivals. Mission schools provided valuable
language skills that improved their ability to trade
with the British. They also hoped that through the
missionaries they could obtain British military
support against their competitors. However, it was
the return of former slaves from Brazil and Sierra
Leone that stimulated the growth in numbers of
native African missionaries, causing Christianity
to really spread in Nigeria.

BISHOP SAMUEL CROWTHER

Samuel Ajayi Crowther was born in Osogun,
Yorubaland. At the age of twelve, in 1821, he
was captured as a slave during the Yoruba Wars
and sold to Portuguese slave traders. The ship
he was on was intercepted by a British naval
patrol, and the slaves on board were taken to
Freetown, Sierra Leone, and released. In 1825
Ajayi was baptized into the Anglican Church
and took the name Samuel Crowther. He
returned to Yorubaland in 1841 as part of the
effort to spread Christianity into the Nigerian
interior. In 1864 he became the first native-
born African bishop of the Anglican Church.

The gradual replacement of the indigenous belief system by Christianity disrupted traditional and communal power and social structures. Christian churches promoted formal education and vocational training, thus creating a new political order in which the educated often had advantages over those favored by the traditional hierarchies. The churches also set out to influence indigenous practices such as polygyny (the marriage of one man to more than one woman), slavery, and sacrifices.

Slavery
Slavery and various forms of bonded labor existed in the territory of Nigeria before the arrival of Europeans. Slaves served primarily as a supplement to paid labor and as such could hold practically any job, from menial and household work to high administrative posts and even important military positions. Slaves normally lived as dependents within their owners' families, and were thus integrated into the larger society. Furthermore, the children of slaves were generally not slaves themselves.

The establishment of plantation labor in the New World in the sixteenth century and the rise of the British and Dutch commercial empires saw a dramatic increase in the trade in slaves—an event that produced massive social and political changes in most communities in Nigeria. In the Bight of Benin, in the southwest, local kings established royal monopolies that competed with one another for European trade. They purchased slaves through middlemen from states in the interior where the slaves were captured through wars or raids. For instance, the city-state of Oyo became one of the largest empires in Nigerian history largely due to its strategic position between the northern trans-Sahel slave trade route and the coastal European trade area.

Further east along the coast into the Bight of Biafra, on the other hand, decentralized political structures allowed the development of powerful commercial interests in the slave trade. In this region slaves were mainly obtained through judicial rulings or kidnappings, or on the order of an oracle who had demanded slaves for a favorable ruling. The rise of powerful local commercial organizations altered the balance of power away from the traditional rulers and social structures.

Abolition

The abolition of the slave trade in 1807 hastened the demise of the powerful Oyo Empire, which was slowly losing territory due to expansionist pressures from the Sokoto Caliphate to the north. Oyo's demise set off what are known as the Yoruba Wars of the nineteenth century, which destabilized much of western Nigeria.

The slave trade gave way to the trade in palm oil, which was valuable in the production of soap, candles, and industrial lubricants. In the Yoruba southwest, the production of palm oil was dominated by large plantations that required huge amounts of labor, particularly female. This industry actually increased the internal demand for (women) slaves. The industry was controlled by warlords whose dominion over their territories was largely outside traditional power structures.

In the southeastern regions of Nigeria, the palm-oil industry was decentralized in primarily family-based small farms. Again, this had a significant impact on women in the region, as most of the work involved in palm-oil production was done by women. Polygyny was a useful economic structure that enabled the increasing participation of women in the local economy.

Colonialism

During the mid-nineteenth century, Great Britain's domination of trade on the Nigerian coast was increasingly threatened by the ambitions of other European countries. The Berlin Conference of 1884–85 set off the "scramble for Africa," during which the British set out to establish a visible power base within the Nigerian territories. In the south the British established treaties of "protection" that varied from region to region to accommodate local traditions and structures. Local leaders signed these treaties in the hope that this would improve their trade position with the British or give them an advantage over their neighbors. In reality, however, they had little choice: the British military crushed any refusal or rebellion swiftly and unconditionally. Once they had gained control of the south, the British turned their attention to the Caliphate in the north.

Here, stiff resistance forced them to overthrow the Caliphate and then capture by force each individual state, a process which took until 1903 to complete.

The British governed their Nigerian colony through "indirect rule." The goal, theoretically, was not to change existing political and social institutions but only to change those customs, traditions, and institutions that were thought to be harmful to Nigerian progress and British commercial interests. In the north, indirect rule was easily implemented: Britain obtained the political and commercial power it wanted, and left the daily administration of the people to the centralized control of the emirs. The lives of ordinary northerners changed very little. In the southern regions, however, a great deal of political change was required of the local systems of administration in order to accommodate the needs of the British Empire. For example, the chiefs appointed by the British became minions

of the colonial power and were no longer perceived as true representatives of the people. Furthermore, the rapid imposition of a cash-based economy caused enormous social upheaval.

In 1914, the Northern and Southern Protectorates were united into the Colony and Protectorate of Nigeria under the first governor-general, Frederick Lugard. His attempts to impose a unified governing structure across the entire area led to large protests in the late 1920s and a burgeoning nationalist movement—the birth of the concept of being "Nigerian." In 1939, the colony was divided into three administrative regions: the Hausa-Fulani/Fulani-dominated north, the Igbo-dominated east, and the Yoruba-dominated west. In 1946, a nationalist struggle led by the educated elite gave rise to a constitutional review (the Richards Constitution) that established Houses of Assembly in the three regions. This period also saw a gradual awareness on the part of the British colonial authorities of the need to support indigenous education, industry, and general development. In 1951 the introduction of elected representation led to the formation of three regional political parties. The Lyttleton Constitution of 1954 established Nigeria as a federation of three regions, plus the federal territory of Lagos (the national capital).

INDEPENDENT NIGERIA: KEY DATES

October 1, 1960 Nigeria gains its independence. Sir Abubakar Tafawa Balewa is the first prime minister; Nnamdi Azikiwe is the first governor-general.

October 1, 1963 Nigeria declares itself a federal republic; Nnamdi Azikiwe is the first president of the First Republic.

January 15, 1966 Failed military coup by leftist southerners kills Balewa; the coup is stopped by other military leaders and General Aguiyi-Ironsi takes over as head of state.

July 29, 1966 Countercoup by northerners places Lieutenant-Colonel Yakubu Gowon (a Christian from the middle belt) as head of state.

May 1967–January1970 Civil War.

July 30, 1975 Military coup places General Murtala Muhammed as head of state.

February 13, 1976 Attempted coup in which General Muhammed is killed. Lieutenant-General Olusegun Obasanjo becomes military ruler.

August 11, 1979 Elections held; Shehu Shagari is elected president of the Second Republic.

August–September 1983 Second elections; Shagari is declared the winner, sparking mass violence because the elections are perceived to be rigged.

December 31, 1983 Military coup places General Muhammandu Buhari as head of state.

August 27, 1985 Military coup places General Ibrahim Babangida as military ruler.

April 22, 1990 Failed coup attempt.

December 12, 1991 The capital is officially moved from Lagos to Abuja.

June 12, 1993 Elections are held and won by Chief Moshood Abiola, but the results are annulled by General Babangida.

August 27, 1993 Strikes, riots, and international pressure force General Babangida to step down and hand power to an interim governing council led by Chief Ernest Shonekan, who is to organize new elections—the Third Republic.

November 17, 1993 General Sani Abacha leads a military coup.

June 12, 1994 Chief Abiola continues to press for his presidential mandate and declares himself president; he is arrested and imprisoned, and dies in prison in 1998.

November 10, 1995 General Abacha has Ken Saro-Wiwa and eight of his people executed.

June 8, 1998 Abacha dies at the age of fifty-four under controversial circumstances; General Abdulsalam Abubakar replaces him and sets up a transition program to return the country to democratic rule.

May 29, 1999 Chief Olusegun Obasanjo is declared the democratically elected president of Nigeria—beginning of the Fourth Republic.

April 21, 2007 Election of Umaru Musa Yar'Adua as president.

May 6, 2010 President Yar'Adua dies; his vice president, Goodluck Jonathan, succeeds to the presidency.

April 2011 Elections held; Goodluck Jonathan reelected president.

Independence

Elections were held in 1959 to determine the makeup of the first independent government, and on October 1, 1960, Nigeria gained its independence. Political governance was fragile, however: the nation was still far from being economically independent, the differences

between rural and urban development were growing, and regional identities and ethnic divisions hardened into political agendas. For example, the British had mainly staffed the armed forces with Muslim northerners but had selected officers from the predominantly Christian south. After independence, the government of President Balewa (a northerner) changed this policy so that 50 percent of the officers were recruited from the north. Also, more funding was funneled to the north for education and health programs—these had been funded in the south by the colonial regime but were far less developed in the north.

These types of policies were meant to balance social and economic opportunities between the three main ethnic groups, but were perceived as favoritism and served to fuel fears of ethnic domination by one group over the others. The federal elections of 1964 were widely regarded as having been grossly rigged by all parties, and strengthened the opinion of many Nigerians that governments in all regions were willing to pursue political power at any cost.

On January 15, 1966, five majors (four of whom were Igbo men from the southwest) led a coup against the civilian government, killing or imprisoning many important members of the political class at the time. Other military leaders thwarted the ambitions of these men and arrested them. Power devolved to the senior military man, Major-General John Aguiyi-Ironsi. With the stated goal of ending corruption and regionalism, Aguiyi-Ironsi abolished the federal system and replaced it with a centralized unitary system.

On July 29, 1966, a group of northern military men carried out a countercoup and installed Colonel Yakubu Gowon as head of state. He reinstated the federal system, but the coup caused a spate of massacres of Igbos living in the north, and revenge killings of northerners in the south.

The Nigerian Civil War, 1967–70

Between 80,000 and 100,000 Igbos lost their lives during the massacres from September 1966 to early 1967, causing large population shifts. Lieutenant Colonel Ojukwu, the Igbo military governor of the Eastern region, considered secession of the Igbo region in southeastern Nigeria, based on the fear that Igbos were no longer safe in the country.

For the federal military government, secession was unthinkable: the breaking away of one region would open the door to the disintegration of the federation. Furthermore, 67 percent of known oil reserves in the country were located in this area. On May 30, 1967, after the breakdown of talks, Ojukwu declared independence for the region as the Republic of Biafra. Federal forces advanced into Biafra in July. The war lasted two and a half years and took the lives of between one and three million Nigerians, many through starvation; as many as three million were displaced. After victory by the federal army, the process of reintegration and reconciliation began immediately, supported by the massive growth in income from petroleum production in the 1970s.

Military Rule
The Nigerian economy grew rapidly during the 1970s, but the wealth created by oil revenues was distributed unequally, benefiting primarily those who had access to state power—and to state resources. The two military regimes and one civilian government of the 1970s had little accountability to the people in the "rentier state" system, in which government revenue is not generated through taxes or internal borrowing but from the licenses granted to and royalties received from multinational petroleum corporations. This system facilitated the development of corruption, a patronage culture, and an ineffective and bloated bureaucracy.

Each military leader in Nigeria has taken over with the declared intention of returning the country to civilian rule, cracking down on corruption, and focusing on the country's economic development—and in each case, their lack of action on these goals has stimulated the next military coup. The world oil surplus of the 1980s threw Nigeria into a recession in the early 1990s and was a major impetus behind the two military coups of the decade. General Buhari was so determined to root out the evil of corruption that his "War Against Indiscipline" turned the country into a police state marked by fear and high inflation for ordinary Nigerians, with continued high-level corruption on the part of those in power.

General Babangida, for his part, began an ambitious program of market reform and flirted with the notion of civilian rule. In 1986 he instituted a structural adjustment program that allowed debt rescheduling and opened new lines of credit. This program had a positive effect on Nigeria's balance sheet but had a devastating impact on the lives of ordinary Nigerians, marked by increased unemployment, rapid inflation, and a continued decline in the quality and availability of social services. Government corruption flourished during this period.

In 1993, General Babangida held the long-promised national elections. Nigerians placed hope for their future in the June 12 elections, which were felt to be genuinely free and fair. Unfortunately, General Babangida annulled the result (won by Chief Moshood Abiola, a Yoruba man from the southwest), setting off months of unrest across the country. Eventually bowing to public pressure, Babangida stepped down, handing power to Chief Ernest Shonekan. However, his annulment of the elections had already set in motion the military coup, three months later, by Sani Abacha, the most notorious and brutal of Nigeria's military rulers. Abacha abolished all political institutions, including the state and national assemblies, governorships, and electoral bodies, and banned all political parties. During his rule, Nigeria became an international pariah state for its curbing of civil freedoms such as freedom of expression, and for ordering the execution of the internationally renowned author and activist Ken Saro-Wiwa. In 1995, Nigeria was suspended from the Commonwealth because of human rights abuses, while the USA and other countries considered imposing sanctions. General Abacha died at the age of fifty-four in 1998, presumably from a heart attack.

The Road Back to Democracy
Elections held on May 29, 1999, were won by ex-General Olusegun Obasanjo, marking the start of the Fourth Republic. In 2003 President Obasanjo was reelected for a second term. A  third presidential election was held on April 21, 2007, with Umaru Yar'Adua winning the vote. Significantly, this was the first peaceful handover of power from one democratically elected leader to another, though the presidential elections of 2003 and 2007 were marred by significant irregularities and violence.

On February 9, 2010, Vice President Goodluck Jonathan was declared acting president by the National Assembly in the absence of President Umaru Yar'Adua, who had been ill since late November 2009. Upon Yar'Adua's death on May 5, 2010, Jonathan succeeded to the presidency. Despite the fact that his primary mandate was limited to overseeing new elections, he pushed a few well-timed reforms through, including electoral reforms, building on the work of the previous governments. On October 1, 2010, Nigeria celebrated its fiftieth anniversary of independence. In elections held in April 2011, President Jonathan was reelected. The election process was regarded nationally and internationally as being free and credible, though there were some cases of attempted fraud, and violence was instigated in areas of the north by disenfranchised youth who were angry that a southerner had been elected. Nonetheless, the elections remain significant: Nigeria is currently experiencing its longest period of civilian rule since its independence.

THE ECONOMY

Nigeria's economy is heavily dependent on oil and gas, which account for approximately 95 percent of its foreign exchange earnings and about 80 percent of government revenue. It is currently the seventh-largest exporter of oil in the world and the eleventh-largest exporter of natural gas.

Since the 1970s, the importance of agriculture, other mineral exploitation, and industrial development has declined. Manufacturing accounts for only about 4 percent of GDP. It is estimated that around 70 percent of the workforce are active in the small farm agricultural sector and in the informal sector in urban areas: roughly 80 percent of the population are self-employed.

There are extreme variations in income distribution. Approximately 20 percent of the population own more than 65 percent of national assets, while well over 60 percent of Nigerians receive an income of less than US$1.25 a day (the World Bank's measure for extreme poverty).

The fact that there are too few employment opportunities in the formal sector has stimulated a brain drain that has seen the out-migration of a hefty portion of Nigeria's highly skilled labor force. According to the Development Research Centre on Migration, Globalisation and Poverty, 14 percent of all Nigerian-trained physicians work abroad, 90 percent of them in the USA and UK. Nigeria's migrants do contribute to the economy of their country, however: remittances from diaspora Nigerians are now estimated to be the country's second-largest foreign exchange earner after petroleum.

While the country still faces significant development issues, it is generally agreed that the successive civilian governments have made important efforts to implement economic reforms, introducing deregulation, improving transparency and accountability, and undertaking privatization programs at the federal level. Over the last few years, the government has begun a process of modernizing the banking system and addressing regional disputes over the distribution of the country's wealth. These programs are starting to have an effect: Nigeria's GDP growth rate was

estimated at 6.7 percent in 2009 and nearly
8 percent in 2010 (only China and India did better
in the same years). This growth has come primarily
from the agricultural, telecommunications, and
manufacturing sectors.

THE LEGAL SYSTEM

The Nigerian legal system is based in part on
English common law and also on customary law,
which is based on the customs and traditions of
the various ethnic groups in the country. Islamic
law is also applied in twelve northern states.

The administration of justice—who is eligible
to try what type of cases—can be mind-bogglingly
complicated. Issues dealing with business

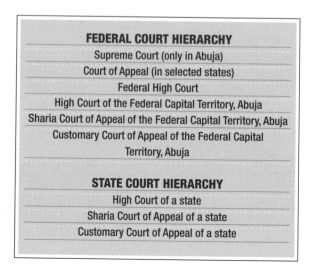

FEDERAL COURT HIERARCHY

Supreme Court (only in Abuja)

Court of Appeal (in selected states)

Federal High Court

High Court of the Federal Capital Territory, Abuja

Sharia Court of Appeal of the Federal Capital Territory, Abuja

Customary Court of Appeal of the Federal Capital
Territory, Abuja

STATE COURT HIERARCHY

High Court of a state

Sharia Court of Appeal of a state

Customary Court of Appeal of a state

contracts will fall under the formal, English-based legal system, which functions as it does in the UK. Both federal and state courts are governed by the Constitution. The minor courts, such as the Magistrate's Court, are governed by state law and fall within the jurisdiction of the attorney general of each state.

GOVERNMENT

Nigeria is a federal republic in which the president is both chief of state and head of the government. He (or she, though there have been no female presidents of Nigeria as yet) is elected by popular vote, under universal suffrage from eighteen years of age, for no more than two four-year terms. He runs the country with his cabinet, the Federal Executive Council.

The country's current constitution dates from 1999, when the first elected president, Olusegun Obasanjo, took office. It defines the functions and services of the three tiers of government: federal, state, and local government. There are currently thirty-six states and one Federal Capital Territory, and 774 local government areas. The states are effectively grouped into six geopolitical zones based loosely on linguistic affinity and cultural affiliation. Policies that aim to balance disbursements or investment decisions within the country are based on these regional divisions.

THE REGIONS AND THEIR STATES
North-central region: Benue, Kogi, Kwara, Nasarawa, Niger, Plateau, and the Federal Capital Territory.
Northeastern region: Adamawa, Bauchi, Borno, Gombe, Taraba, and Yobe.
Northwestern region: Jigawa, Kaduna, Kano, Katsina, Kebbi, Sokoto, and Zamfara.
Southeastern region: Abia, Anambra, Ebonyi, Enugu, and Imo.
South-south region: Akwa Ibom, Bayelsa, Cross River, Delta, Edo, and Rivers (also known as the Niger Delta region).
Southwestern region: Ekiti, Lagos, Ogun, Ondo, Osun, and Oyo.

The legislative branch of government is similar to that found in the American system. In the bicameral National Assembly, the Senate has 109 seats (three from each state plus one from Abuja).

Members are elected by popular vote to serve four-year terms. The House of Representatives has 360 seats; its members are also elected by popular vote to serve four-year terms.

The responsibilities of the federal and state governments are written into the Constitution, but tensions do exist: since independence there has been a tendency to decentralize power in favor of the states. For instance, Lagos State has created its own traffic police corps outside the federal force. In terms of income, the federal government controls receipts from oil, corporation taxes, and other duties and levies. The states get a portion of the oil receipts as distributed by the federal government, and also levy personal income tax. In Lagos this is an important part of the budget, but it is negligible for many other states.

In terms of responsibilities, the federal government is in charge of overarching issues such as national infrastructure, ports, airports, the police and military, and foreign policy. The states are responsible for most service provision, such as primary education and local roads.

One of the main issues has always been how to divide the income from oil between the federal and state levels, as well as among the states themselves. Currently, approximately 25 percent of the federal annual budget goes to the salaries of the National Assembly. The funds that are distributed to the states are calculated based on a complex system that provides, for instance, an extra disbursement to the oil-producing states. However, there is a common view in the Niger

Delta (oil-producing) region that the wealth created there is not reinvested in the region, a perception that is aggravated by widespread corruption at the state government level. Poverty, unemployment, and underdevelopment have encouraged locals to resort to the unsafe tapping of pipelines for free oil, which results in spills and explosions and has led to environmental degradation. Today, the violence and sabotage that takes place in the region is largely attributed to international crime syndicates that profit from the black market trade in illegally "bunkered" oil. Yar'Adua's government negotiated a fragile peace agreement with rebels in the Delta Region, which reduced the fighting, kidnappings, and sabotage that had crippled the industry and reduced production by 25 percent. Future policies will determine whether the region remains stable.

NIGERIA IN THE WORLD TODAY

Nigeria is a member of OPEC and the British Commonwealth. For the 2010–11 term, it had a non-permanent seat on the UN Security Council. Unfortunately its international reputation is tarnished by the stories of violence and kidnappings in the Delta region, by the religious clashes that occur in particular cities in the middle-belt region, and by the criminal activities of a few of its nationals, such as "419 scams" (fraudulent e-mails sent around the world with promises of huge profits if you first pay a deposit into a certain account) and the illegal trafficking of young women and girls into prostitution. However, the success of individual Nigerians in areas such as sports, music, and literature is a far more positive, if less well known, achievement.

Nigeria is a strong regional player: it is a leading member of the New Partnership for African Development (NEPAD), the African Union (AU), and the African Peer Review Mechanism (APRM). It also plays a prominent role in UN peacekeeping missions and mediation in West Africa (Liberia, Sierra Leone, Togo) and elsewhere in Africa (Sudan). It took a firm stand against Cote d'Ivoire strongman Laurent Gbagbo, in line with Western countries, in 2011. It also supported NATO air strikes against Libya, which few of its neighbors were willing to do. With its current economic growth rate, political stability, and foreign policy approach, Nigeria aims to be nothing less than a world power.

The main hurdles Nigeria faces are its over-dependence on oil revenues; the effects of cross-border organized crime, such as people, narcotics, and weapons trafficking; and the historic underfunding of the education sector. There is today a strong feeling of hope for the future, fueled partly by the work of a few key people in government and partly by the growth of an educated and vocal middle class anxious for true stability and development. That said, many Nigerians continue to face extreme difficulties in their daily lives. Improvements will require less corruption, better education, and an enabling economic environment across the country.

chapter two

VALUES &
ATTITUDES

Nigerian culture varies greatly according to ethnic group, urban or rural location, religious beliefs, and levels of education. Over the past fifty years of the country's existence, however, a (mainly urban) Nigerian identity has developed that acknowledges the many distinct cultural traditions but is informed by a shared experience of the nation's historical development, and by the common struggle to succeed in everyday life. Nonetheless, today most Nigerians still identify first with their family, then with their community, which is highly influenced by their religion and ethnic group, and finally, more vaguely, with their nation.

ATTITUDES TO LIFE

The first thing one notices about Nigerians is their open cheerfulness. This good spirit is expressed differently by each ethnic group—the Yoruba in the southwest may be the most gregarious, and the Hausa-Fulani in the north the most restrained—but across the country, Nigerians smile and laugh, partly because it is expected social behavior as well as being a way of dealing with adversity. Nigerians have a fundamentally positive attitude to life. On the one hand, they tend to be fatalistic: "It is God's will" or "God willing" are commonly heard expressions. On the other, their fatalism is based on an optimistic vision of the future: if they work hard and do their best, things can only get better. They are therefore proactive and pragmatic in their approach to getting what they want. In fact, the Nigerian spirit is remarkable: they remain good-humored, work hard, and build a good life for themselves *despite* a system that seems stacked against them. Confronted by the struggle of everyday life, Nigerians are tireless and stoical—they may like to complain, but they tend to get on with the hard business of getting by.

FAMILY VALUES

Across all of Nigeria's disparate cultures, the family is the pillar and the most important unit of society. Being part of a family provides an individual with his or her communal identity, social status, and financial safety net. Therefore, to be married and have children is the ultimate goal of practically all Nigerians. To be unmarried or not to have children is to be unlucky, somehow "defective," or simply eccentric—it is, to a certain extent, to be ostracized from the normal activities and roles of daily life. For many Nigerians, it is inconceivable that one would *choose* not to get married or not to have children. Perhaps this helps to explain why homosexuality is still illegal in Nigeria under federal law.

In the Nigerian context, the family is the extended, not the nuclear, family. This includes a matriarch and patriarch (and all of their brothers and sisters, aunts, uncles, and so on), their children and their male children's wives, and the grandchildren. The family network replaces the welfare state—those who earn more are expected to help the others when need dictates. In a country with such high unemployment, those with steady jobs receive regular requests for financial assistance for everything from school fees to business propositions. Furthermore, given the current economic conditions in the country, it is not a foregone conclusion that children will become independent. Male children, therefore, may live with, and depend on, their parents long into their adult lives.

There are rather strict rules that dictate the roles and behavior of individuals within the family. Extended family members can and do influence the lives of individual couples—no family arguments remain private for long. Though norms and expectations vary according to ethnic group, they always include rules that define the way to show deference to one's elders. Nigerian family values can be described as Victorian in that there are strict codes of social etiquette and rigid definitions of "acceptable" relationships and behavior and the roles prescribed to men and women. Parents want to know who their children socialize with, and the behavior of "the Joneses" is observed and commented on.

THE VALUE OF MARRIAGE

A marriage in Nigeria is not just the union of two individuals, but the bringing together of two families—a very important event with ramifications that extend beyond the individuals involved. Because the bride goes to join her husband's

family, the mother-in-law is a formidable central personage in an extended family. In big cities like Lagos and Abuja, mixed marriages are not unheard of—between branches of Christianity, between Muslims and Christians, and between ethnic groups. Urban women tend to marry later in life than rural women. Arranged marriages still occur in Muslim regions, occasionally even for girls under the age of sixteen.

Practically all family structures are male dominated and patrilineal. Men, therefore, have more formal power within the family structure than women. Polygyny (where one man is allowed to marry more than one woman) is still practiced in much of Nigeria: polyandry (where women are allowed to marry more than one husband) is not permitted. Polygyny is allowed by the Muslim religion and is also common under traditional belief systems. Christian men who belong to some of the independent African churches can also marry more than one wife. In the urban, Christian south of the country, monogamy is far more common today.

Yoruba families tend to be looser than those of other ethnic groups. A husband in a polygynous marriage may live part-time with one or another of his wives; even in monogamous marriages, men and women tend to have separate social lives and each their own busy career. It is fairly accepted (or at least cynically expected) that men who can afford it have mistresses whom they maintain financially. On the other hand, it is not socially acceptable for women to have extramarital affairs. It would be misplaced to assume that all Nigerians always adhere to social expectations, however—after all, men could not have mistresses if all women were locked into socially acceptable relationships. This is an example of how Nigerian norms and values are tempered by a pragmatic attitude to dealing with life's realities.

GENDER ROLES

Men exert broad control over the lives of women and there are strict divisions between gender roles, though these vary across ethnic groups. Generally, women raise the children and therefore pass down cultural values, attitudes, norms, and behavior to future generations. Traditionally, women are expected to be polite, mild mannered, even tempered, and obedient to their husbands, but Nigerian women tend not to be passively subservient. They are often powerful forces to contend with, both within their families and in their communities. For example, local politicians understand the importance of obtaining the support of market women's collectives because of the role they play in influencing community opinions.

In the Muslim north, men are ideally the main wage earners, the heads of the household, and are responsible for the security, safety, and well-being of the family. In rural areas the men do the farming, and in the cities they are the traders and market sellers. Women's place is in the home managing the household. The status of Muslim women in Nigeria is similar to that in other Islamic countries, with all the variety that that implies. Hausa-Fulani Muslims have as an ideal the total seclusion of women (*purdah*), which is practiced by those who can afford it. Less wealthy women, however, may have to work and therefore go out to, for instance, help with the farming or work as domestics in wealthier homes. Many women in *purdah* do take up economic activities: they may

trade in foodstuffs or crafts that they make, or become middlemen in the trade of other articles. They use children or brothers or palace workers as couriers or intermediaries for their business. They invest their personal wealth in jewelry.

Muslim women in the south are more emancipated than northerners; they do not wear a head scarf, and their daily lives are similar to those of their ethnically related Christian sisters. In Abuja and the south, elite Muslim women are well educated, can become doctors, lawyers, and the like, and can own their own businesses.

In Christian communities, women have traditionally played a larger economic role in the family. Ideally, Yoruba women are expected to have an income independent from their husbands: husbands provide a home and a household budget as well as the funds to set the wife up in her business dealings. Most Yoruba women work—as market traders, farm laborers, business owners—and they can be found in all the urban professions, including government positions. Their money pays for their upkeep and that of their children; many children have been educated through the toil of their mothers.

Igbo men marry later than in other ethnic groups because they want to secure a job and a home before taking on the responsibility of a family, for whom they are expected to be the main income earner. While Igbo women are expected to be homemakers, proportionally more Igbo women are educated to higher levels than other women in the country.

WOMEN'S RIGHTS

The Constitution guarantees equal rights for women. Nigerian women obtained the right to vote in 1978; they can drive, have equal property and inheritance rights, and have equal access to public services such as education. However, traditional practices can prevent women from fully benefiting from these rights. Across the country, urban women, especially those in the upper social classes, have better access to quality education, health services, job opportunities, and inheritance rights than their rural sisters.

An example of this strain between tradition and national laws is inheritance rights, particularly when a woman is widowed. Under Nigeria's formal legal system (and its obligations under the Convention on the Elimination of all forms of Discrimination against Women, CEDAW), women have equal inheritance rights with men. However, custom in all of Nigeria's ethnic groups has limited a wife's access to her husband's estate, which generally reverts to his

family. Thus a widow can be left homeless and penniless should her in-laws be so inclined.

A woman's recourse to justice depends on her awareness of her formal rights and her financial means to gain access to the courts. Furthermore, the administration of justice in Nigeria is generally slow and expensive. The risk is that by the time a woman has established her rights, her husband's estate will effectively have already been distributed among his family members.

COMMUNITY VALUES

In Nigeria, an individual's identity is much more strongly influenced by the community than it is in the West. Nigerians are keenly aware of belonging to an ethnic group that is defined by its internal culture and history and by its differences from other ethnic groups; however, it is safe to say that Nigerians are among the most individualistic people in Africa in terms of their strength of character and the highly competitive nature of modern Nigerian society.

Within the community, an individual's identity or status is determined by seniority (the older the better) and gender (men are higher up than women), as well as the family's wealth, lineage, and traditional role (such as with hereditary titles). Today, an individual's occupation and personal wealth are also important. Outside her work environment, a woman's position in her community is related to her family-in-law's status and how many (male) children she has.

Nigerian society is therefore not egalitarian: knowing one's place in the natural order of social hierarchies is important. Being polite and showing respect to people higher up the hierarchy is expected and is seen as a sign of good social behavior. If someone puts on airs, they will be sharply reminded of their place.

Relationships
Each community is linked through an intricate system of personal relationships that includes friendships, work contacts, and patronage links. Financial success brings a responsibility to care for others; it also confers power and prestige on the giver. There is a great deal of formal respect and deference given to an *oga*, or "big man" (a wealthy and powerful individual).

As in the West, the term "friend" can define a wide variety of relationships, from close friendships formed in childhood to loose acquaintance-type friendships. However, a Nigerian cannot have an *equal* relationship (arguably the true definition of friendship) with anyone who is two or three years older or younger than themselves. A close friend is part of an individual's support network—they will be willing and able to help out in times of need.

Within this system of relationships, foreigners are generally seen benignly as outsiders who can potentially become an asset or even, over time, a "friend." However, the large income and power differential between foreigners and most Nigerians—all except a thin sliver of the wealthy

class—means that it is up to the foreigner to
earn the trust and friendship of Nigerians.

Charity and mutual support among Nigerians
is not limited to the family and community
network. Many wealthy individuals, either directly
or through organizations such as church groups,
support schools, orphanages, health centers, and
so on. Such local philanthropy helps address the
poverty issues of some of the country's neediest.

RELIGION

Nigerians are deeply religious, and most actively
practice their faith. Organized religions not
only offer hope for the future as people endure
hardships in their daily lives, but also provide
social services such as health and education
where government services have failed.

Indigenous Religions

Indigenous African religions provide a global
framework of life that permeates every situation
and governs traditional society. These belief
systems link each individual with both the
ancestors and future generations, and with the
natural and spirit worlds, in order to ensure the
prosperity of the land for the common good.
In other words, everything is religious.

While specific beliefs vary, Nigeria's indigenous
belief systems have in common a supreme being,
deities that are associated with particular elements
of the environment, and spiritual entities that are
the link between Man and God. Rituals, prayer,

and ceremonies are performed by priests and priestesses who are believed to possess the ability to heal, tell the future, and appeal directly to the deities in the spirit world. These practices are seen to be the key to health and prosperity because spirits can provide protection from evil. The practice of these beliefs reinforces loyalty to communal values and the authority of the elders.

Only 10 percent of Nigeria's population claims to continue to adhere to traditional belief systems. However, while it may not be overtly practiced, belief in the power of the spirit world remains strong among all Nigerians regardless of their Christian or Muslim faith. Even among the highly educated, the power of juju (or supernatural forces) cannot be discounted. Stories occasionally appear in the newspapers about "witch children" or the sacrifice of albinos for juju purposes. While it is acknowledged by many that such practices persist in Nigeria, few admit to believing in them.

Christianity
In the southeast of the country, most of the Catholics are Igbo. In the southwest the Christians are mainly Protestants, including Anglicans, Methodists, Lutherans, and Baptists. Churches form the central point of the congregation's daily life; people attend mass at least once a week and are involved in social projects such as church-led schools or fund-raising for the needy.

Nigeria also has many independent African churches, such as the Cherubim and Seraphim Church, which incorporate African cultural practices with Christianity. Some Pentecostal churches preach a "prosperity gospel" in which God grants wealth and health to believers who have enough faith.

Islam
Nigeria's Muslims are mostly devout but relatively tolerant—the burka is not worn by women, "honor" killings are unknown, and female circumcision is uncommon. Most female children wear a head scarf from when they begin to walk (not at puberty). Non-Muslims are not bound by Sharia law (a God-given code that governs all aspects of religious, political, social, domestic, and private life) anywhere in Nigeria.

The Sharia law implemented in Nigeria is a moderate form. Beginning in 1999, it has been applied in nine Muslim-majority states and in

those regions of three other states where large groups of Muslims live. The introduction of Sharia was popular in the north because it was hoped that it would end injustice, inequality, and corruption, the legal system adopted from the British at independence having been experienced by many as being corrupt and ineffective. The hoped-for improvements in people's lives have not occurred, however, and the fear now is that frustrated youth will turn to radical Islam in their search for justice. This was the case in 2009 when a radical sect called Boko Haram attacked security forces, triggering violence that killed more than seven hundred people.

Attitudes to Others Outside the Community
One aspect of Nigerian society that is quickly clear to outsiders is that there is an acute lack of trust and a deep suspicion on the part of Nigerians toward their compatriots. This is partly due to the intense competition for scarce

resources in the country, for everything from places at good schools to jobs and bank loans: everyone is out to ensure that they and theirs get what they need. There is, practically speaking, no public safety net, which means that what individuals obtain they do so through their own resourcefulness and determination. Furthermore, interethnic suspicions have been encouraged by political maneuverings since independence: politicians appear to have been bent on improving the lot of their fellow tribesmen over the good of the whole of Nigeria.

Nigeria attracts attention when intercommunal violence leads to bloodshed. These conflicts are often portrayed as the result of interethnic or religious hatred, but this interpretation is too simplistic. In most of the country, people of different ethnic and religious backgrounds intermingle, intermarry, and study and work together. In Lagos and Abuja, mosques stand yards away from churches, and no clash has ever occurred.

The deadly violence occurs mainly in the middle-belt region of the country, where large groups of different ethnicities and religions live side by side and where there are underlying struggles over land ownership and political power. For example, in certain states, the registration of "indigenes" or natives of that state (a definition open to dispute) regulates who has access to jobs, government services, land, and so forth. Clashes result when one group feels disadvantaged at the hands of the group in power. Violence can also be triggered by national or international incidents,

such as the 2001 clashes in Kano, which were
sparked when Muslims protesting US air strikes
against Afghanistan went on the rampage.
Media reports give the impression that riots are
widespread, but in reality they are generally
limited to specific areas or neighborhoods.

NATIONAL VALUES AND ATTITUDES

Frequent stories of corruption and self-
enrichment have fed a cynical view of power and
politics. Ministries and government departments
don't trust each other to act in the nation's best
interests; the government doesn't trust the private
sector, and vice versa. Rather than creating a state
of stalemate and discontent, however, all of this
mistrust is tempered by Nigerian pragmatism.
Since the reestablishment of democracy, this has
translated into a society of negotiation and careful
networking, of deals and cross-checks. This may
slow down the process of governing, but it has
recently led to the establishment of more
transparent and broadly supported governing
structures at the federal level.

It may seem contradictory given the level of
cynicism toward their leaders, but Nigerians are
proud of their country and yearn to see it achieve
the power and recognition they feel it deserves.
Nigerians abroad tend to remain in close contact
with their country even if they are away for
decades; not only do they keep in touch with
family and friends, but they stay informed on
political, social, and economic developments.

ATTITUDES TO CORRUPTION

Yes, there is widespread corruption in Nigeria, and many individuals try to gain advantage over others through means that are illegitimate, illegal, or immoral. Corruption takes many forms, from patronage and nepotism to bribery, fraud, and the gross misappropriation of funds. Everyone in Nigeria agrees that corruption is a major problem for the development of the country—it is probably the most common topic in the media.

In discussing corruption, two points must be kept in mind. First, corruption occurs everywhere in the world—from small-scale, individual tax evasion to large corporate or government expenses scandals. In other words, this is not a uniquely Nigerian phenomenon, and there is nothing inherently "corrupt" about Nigerians. Second, there are individuals and institutions in Nigeria that have a solid reputation for integrity, and many who fight corruption on a daily basis. The actions of certain key government officials at the state and national levels have made significant inroads in improving transparency and decreasing the opportunities for corrupt practices, and there is a feeling among many that small steps are being taken in the right direction. However, it is true that the scale of the task means that more work is needed before the country can rise in the rankings of international corruption or good governance lists.

There are two kinds of corruption that are viewed differently by Nigerians. The first is government and public-sector corruption. It is widely accepted among Nigerians that many public officials use their positions to enrich themselves—whether proven or not, the rumor mill has it that they are "all stealing the country blind." Scandals regularly come to light in the papers; for instance, the governor of the Central Bank of Nigeria's declaration that National Assembly members receive around one-quarter of the country's total annual budget in salaries and benefits was hotly denied by the members in question. The Nigerian media reacted with outrage, but were not surprised by the revelation. Whether true or not, many Nigerians saw this as further proof that their national and state leaders lack the skills and moral authority to lead the nation.

The second type of corruption occurs on an everyday level, and here people are more ambivalent. For instance, if someone uses their position or network to get a job or a place in a school for a relative, this may be seen as being a loyal family member in Nigeria's patron-client social system rather than as being corrupt. In some cases, such as the paying of "dashes" or small bribes to officials, most people recognize these officials as corrupt, but many simply give in and pay rather than deal with the inconvenience and irritation of battling the system.

An example of the duality with which corruption is viewed in Nigeria is the infamous "419 scams" (named after the article in Nigerian law that regulates fraud), also known as advance-fee fraud. While these scams are not uniquely Nigerian, the frequency of Nigerian involvement in them has meant that they have become thought of as a Nigerian phenomenon. The schemes take many forms, but the basic idea is to get (largely) foreigners to part with substantial amounts of money. The first to appear were schemes in which a Nigerian claimed to have access to government projects or promised huge returns to anyone willing to help them "unblock" the funds or start up a project by first disbursing large sums of money. Another scam is a dating scheme that sometimes takes many months to set up. In this case, a scammer establishes a relationship via the Internet and eventually requests money for a variety of things: a sick relative, travel costs, education fees, and so on. Sometimes he pretends to be of a nationality other than Nigerian and then claims to be in trouble in Nigeria and in need of money to resolve the issue. As one plan becomes overused, the scammers invent new stories to convince their victims.

Nigerians view the 419 scams with mixed feelings. On the one hand, they regard those who fall for these get-rich-quick schemes as being no better than the scammers themselves, for their loss is the consequence of their own greed and gullibility. While the scammers are recognized as undertaking illegal activities, those who make huge amounts of money (and there are many) are viewed with a mixture of scorn and a certain level of respect for their ingenuity and perseverance. In some cases these fraudsters become "godfathers" in their communities, in which case the means by which their wealth was acquired is conveniently overlooked.

Nigerians, then, are very aware of the shortcomings of their country and are usually unrestrained in their criticism of what is wrong. They know how their country is perceived internationally and are aggrieved by the negative images promoted by the world's media. They are painfully conscious of the legacy of colonialism and the fact that Africans have been seen as second-rate world citizens for the past two centuries. In essence, while Nigerians are highly self-critical, they are proud of their culture and heritage and acutely sensitive to criticism by outsiders.

ATTITUDES TO SUCCESS

If there is any one description that defines Nigerians collectively, it is their ambitiousness and entrepreneurialism. Nigerians aspire to a modern lifestyle and work hard to get it. Those who achieve a certain level of comfort are sure to show it: ostentation—in the sense of showing off what you have earned or achieved—is part of Nigerian culture. Big homes, big cars, big offices, and big jewelry are all signs of success.

Clothing in Nigeria is therefore not just an expression of personal taste: it symbolizes religious affiliation, wealth, and social standing. For this reason, Nigerians spend a lot of money on their clothes and are extremely fashion conscious. Northern women, for example, wear their wealth in jewelry. What you wear and how you look is entirely related to the sense of pride you have in yourself— Nigerians always look smart.

NIGERIAN DRESS SENSE

Nigerians are style conscious and always well dressed, no matter what their economic standing or home conditions. Each region has its traditional dress style, and each type of material has a specific name. In general, Nigerians wear bold and colorful materials. In Abuja, most government officials wear traditional dress. The most basic men's wear is a pair of loose trousers and a long-sleeved, smock-type top, sometimes with a long robe over it. For women the traditional and most common type of dress is the wrapper. Six yards (5.5 meters) of material is cut into three parts: one piece makes the skirt, another makes a blouse, and the last, smallest piece is used as a head tie or to tie a child to one's back.

In the urban south as well as in well-to-do Abuja, many people wear Western clothing, particularly those who work in the private sector. People generally frown upon showing "too much flesh": women can wear slacks or trousers in urban areas, though most Nigerian women wear skirts or dresses, but miniskirts or tight-fitting outfits that reveal too much are not appreciated. Special occasions always mandate dressing up—for example, Sunday at church will be a fashion show affair where many ladies will don stunning head ties folded in elaborate patterns.

ATTITUDES TO EDUCATION

It is probably safe to say that a majority of Nigerian parents see the benefits of education for the advancement of their children, but the parents' economic means, religious background, and own educational level will ultimately influence whether a child goes to school or not.

Historically, the ruling Hausa-Fulani placed little importance on educating the masses. Islamic education was for the elite, and only later for ordinary citizens. The British colonial policy of indirect rule did not interfere with this practice and therefore did not stimulate Western education in northern Nigeria. As a result, literacy, as well as the number of children in school in the north, lags behind in comparison to the south. Both Koranic and regular public schools exist in Muslim communities across the country.

Since the time of the Christian mission schools, southern Nigerians have regarded education as a means of advancement: families spend a significant part of their resources on educating their children. The Igbos are seen as the ethnic group most willing to make sacrifices to educate their children. In Igboland, there is an interesting bias toward educating girls. Men are the economic providers, but because of a lack of formal-sector jobs, many leave school to become entrepreneurs, starting up their own business or joining a family enterprise. Further education is less valued in this context. Girls, on the other hand, are educated to higher levels in order to earn perhaps lower but stable salaries as professionals.

chapter three

CUSTOMS & TRADITIONS

There are various traditional cultural milestones in the yearly calendar, linking Nigerians with their historical and spiritual past. Many of these events have survived the upheavals of colonialism and are seen as important to social cohesion and cultural pride in modern-day Nigeria.

HOLIDAYS

National holidays, both religious and secular, are determined by the federal government. Apart from the religious aspect of these days, they present an opportunity to do nothing. They are valued because most people have very little time off.

Muslim holidays are scheduled according to the moon, and the dates in Nigeria may differ from those in other Muslim countries. The date of a holiday is confirmed only after the federal government declares it to be an official holiday—and this can occur up to the day before the event.

In addition to the dates given opposite, each state can declare its own public holidays. There are a few other special days, such as Children's Day (May 27), in which schools nationwide are closed but banks and offices remain open.

NATIONAL PUBLIC HOLIDAYS	
New Year's Day	January 1
Id el-Moulud (Mawlid in Arabic) Birth of the Prophet Muhammad	Dates vary
Good Friday and Easter Monday	Dates vary
Labor Day	May 1
Democracy Day	May 29
Id el-Fitri (Eid ul-Fitr in Arabic) Celebrates the end of Ramadan	Dates vary
National Day	October 1
Sallah (Id el-Kabir in Arabic) Festival of Sacrifice	Dates vary
Christmas Day	December 25
Boxing Day	December 26

FESTIVALS

Nigeria's customs and traditions can be experieced directly in the rich variety of local festivals that dot the yearly calendar. They celebrate important events in a community's life cycle, such as the harvest, the inauguration or passing of a chief, traditional religious events, and initiation ceremonies. Festivals are crowded, energetic, and colorful, and often have a musical or parade component. Some remain true to tradition, while others are changing to adapt to modern circumstances. A few of the more notable and well visited are mentioned here.

Durbars

A durbar is a formal, public reception or military parade at the court of the traditional ruler in

northern Nigeria. The durbar festivals mix Hausa-
Fulani, Islamic, and colonial traditions into a
colorful, multiday event. The largest durbars
today are held in Katsina and Kano (the largest of
all), and celebrate special events such as the yearly
Muslim festivals of Id el-Kabir (known as Sallah
in Nigeria), the inauguration of new emirs, and
the honoring of visiting heads of state or
government. Festivities include a day of prayer in
a large outdoor arena outside the city and a royal
picnic and procession during which the emir pays
homage to the state governor (a practice that
began in the early twentieth century under British
colonial rule).

The most spectacular event is the procession
of horsemen in which the state's traditional
titleholders, including nobility and district,
village, and ward heads, come to pay homage to
the emir. This practice dates back two centuries to

the time when warfare was waged on horseback.
During this event, thousands of beautifully
dressed riders on decorated horses march through
the city streets to the public square in front of the
emir's palace, where they take their place to await
the arrival of the emir. Musicians, dancers, and
acrobats accompany the groups of horsemen,
adding to the excitement of the thousands of
watchers lining the road.

At the end of the procession, the emir arrives
on horseback, protected from the sun by a large
parasol and surrounded by his regimental guards.
He takes his place in a corner of the parade
grounds. Each group of horsemen then charges
at full speed toward the emir, screaming, spears
raised, only to stop a few feet in front of him and
salute. This is accompanied by the firing of the
incredibly loud rifles of the royal gunmen, who
are nearly knocked off balance with the kickback
of the shot. The festival ends with the return of
the emir to his palace and the slow dissolution
of the boisterous crowds.

Argungu Festival

Argungu is a riverside town in Kebbi State, in
Nigeria's far northwest. Once a year, around
February/March, the town hosts a four-day festival
that marks the end of the growing season and the
beginning of the harvest. This lively festival began
in 1934 as a tribute to the end of centuries of
hostilities between the Sokoto Caliphate and the
Kebbi kingdom. It includes a noisy night market,
canoe racing, donkey and camel races, parades,

wild duck hunting, diving competitions, boxing matches, and musical performances.

The main attraction, however, is the fishing competition that takes place on the last day. Thousands of local men and boys wearing T-shirts and shorts, or just shorts, line the banks of the Matan Fada River armed only with calabash gourds, traditional nets, and their bare hands. At the sound of a gun, they run into the river to try to catch the largest fish. They have one hour, egged on by frenetic drummers in canoes and aided by men with large seed-filled gourds who try to herd the fish into shallow water. This one-mile (1.6-km) stretch of river is protected throughout the year and only accessible on this day.

At the end, the fish are hauled onto scales and weighed. One year, the winning fish weighed seventy-five kilos and it took four people to haul it onto the scales. The competitor with the biggest fish gets big cash and other prizes (which have in the past included a bus) that are donated by the sponsors of the event. Women were originally allowed to participate in the fishing festival, but in recent years, with the tightening of Sharia law, the competition—including the audience—has become virtually all male.

Eyo Festival

The Eyo festival is specific to Lagos Island in Lagos city. The weeklong celebration honors the passing of an important individual in Lagos society, such as an *oba* (king) or other chief or dignitary of the city. As such, the festival is held irregularly, sometimes with many years between events.

The Eyo festival is "played" like a theatrical production over a six-day period and entails secret rites and ceremonies at the shrine of the *eyo* (spirits of the ancestors). The last day of festivities, a Saturday, features a loud and jubilant public procession through the streets of Lagos Island accompanied by music, drummers, singing, and dancing. The parade participants who "play" *eyo* become spirits of the ancestors of Lagos who return to cleanse the city of evil, paving the way for the city's future prosperity. The *eyo* surround and protect one of the five *orisas* (beings somewhat like minor gods) who lead the procession; each wears a different colored hat, the *aga* (white for the senior *orisa*, red, yellow, green, and purple for the others), and each is followed by a group of similarly dressed *eyo* players.

Each *eyo* wears a white robe, the *agbada*, and their faces are covered in a veil of cream-colored

asha-oke (traditional, handwoven cotton material); they wear wide-brimmed hats and are barefoot. They hold the *opambata*, the stick that is used to bless onlookers or to smack those who break the rules of Eyo: you must not wear shoes, smoke, wear a hat, or use an umbrella in the presence of an *orisa*.

The procession is always accompanied by a coffin, representing the deceased, and an old man who is a malevolent spirit and is feared—he is not supposed to be gazed upon, and no photos should be taken of him (any that are will mysteriously fail to come out!). While the festival is a happy one, the crowds traditionally fear the lead *orisa*, known as Adimu. When he passes, people click their fingers over their shoulders, a gesture that means "this can't hurt me." The procession ends in the late afternoon at the football (soccer) stadium, where throngs of visitors will have gathered to view the spectacle.

Osun Festival
The Osun festival is a highlight of the Yoruba calendar, attended by thousands and televised to millions. The festival is held toward the end of the rainy season (August/September) in the Sacred Forest near the town of Oshogbo in the heart of Yorubaland. It pays homage to Osun, the Yoruba goddess of fertility and the Osun River, an important deity in the Yoruba religion. Devotees, traditionally wearing white clothes, bring food offerings and make libations. The highlight of the festival is the procession to the

main shrine, where a ceremony is held that
celebrates the life force of the river.

New Yam Festival
The New Yam festival is held by Igbo
communities at the end of the rainy season in
August to mark the beginning of the yam
harvest season. The yam is a basic food staple
in Nigeria—a good harvest heralds a good year
ahead for the community.

The festival itself varies according to local
custom, but generally the tradition will entail the
throwing out of any remaining yams from the
previous year. A ritual offering is then made to
the gods and ancestors, an act performed either
by the oldest man in the community or a chief
or king. A feast of yam dishes is shared among
the community and its guests, accompanied by
a rowdy celebration with music, dance, singing,
and laughter.

FAMILY CELEBRATIONS AND EVENTS
When Nigerians celebrate, they do so in style.
Important family events include weddings,
funerals, a child's first birthday party, wedding
anniversaries, commemorations of those who
have passed on, and special birthdays such as
the fiftieth and seventieth. These will likely be
big events, where hundreds of guests enjoy
food, live music, and a boisterous atmosphere
replete with long speeches and perhaps a
professional master of ceremonies.

Weddings

Weddings are a major opportunity for celebration
in Nigeria. The exact process of getting married
varies according to ethnic group, how modern or
traditional the families involved are, the families'
religious beliefs, and their financial means.
Weddings can be civil, religious, or traditional.
Most Nigerians continue to have a traditional
African wedding as well as a religious ceremony:
Muslims will have a *nikai* in a mosque, and
Christians will have a church ceremony. These
may or may not be held on the same day and are
seen as separate events.

A traditional African wedding is more than just
the marriage ceremony—it is a long process that
begins when a young man and woman indicate
to their respective families their desire to marry.
Arranged marriages do still occur in rural areas,
but they are not the norm. Each family undertakes
a "due diligence" of the prospective in-laws. These
days a family could still refuse their child's choice

of partner, but in general there will be a good reason for this refusal. Depending on local and family customs, one or more members of each family will meet at least once to discuss the details of the wedding. These meetings can be informal or, as in the past, well choreographed and steeped in local traditions (who says what to whom, and when) and rituals, such as the sharing of the kola nut (who breaks it, the order in which people are served, when it is done).

During these meetings the families get to know one another and decide on such details as the date and particulars of the ceremony, as well as the "bride price." In most of Nigeria, the bride price is merely symbolic: it can be as little as 20 naira (0.01 cents). Often during the official ceremony, the bride's father will give it to the bride herself, or return the money to the groom's family, indicating that "our daughter is not for sale." The bride's family generally pays for the wedding itself and provides food and drink to the groom's family during their pre-wedding visits. They will also provide their daughter with the things that she needs to set up her home, which can include an oven, linens, crockery, and so on. The groom's family will provide a previously agreed-upon list of gifts to the bride's family; this normally includes several reams of cloth, jewelry, food and drink, and in certain ethnic groups, even larger items such as a car.

On the day of the traditional wedding, the families and invited guests will gather at the home of the bride or in a rented hall. In each ethnic group there is a protocol for greeting the important members of each family. The bride will be in another room and once the formalities of greetings are over and everyone is settled with a drink, the guests will request that "their" bride be brought out. In the Yoruba tradition, the bride's family will pretend to trick the in-laws by bringing out a false bride (their heads are covered), to the loud refusal of the groom's family. This may happen a few times before the real bride is brought out and then kneels in front of the groom's parents. She then sits next to her fiancé and is offered a ring and either a Bible or the Koran. She accepts the holy book and ring, at which point the couple are declared married.

In the Igbo tradition, the bride comes out when she is first called and goes to greet the guests and the groom's family. Her father will give her a cup of palm wine; she will take it and then go in search of the groom, who is hiding in the crowd. When she finds him, she kneels in front of him, drinks from the cup of palm wine and passes it to him, and then they are married.

Now the party can start. The size of the party depends on the financial means of the bride's family. It will entail a lot of food, live music, possibly a master of ceremonies, and photographers. Groups of friends and family provide the guests with small gifts as a memento; these can be anything from plastic bowls to leather wallets or useful household items. A particularity of a traditional Nigerian wedding is that instead of throwing rice at the married couple, Nigerians throw money. This tradition is known as "spraying"—as the couple dances, the guests will throw (small denomination) bills at them to wish them success and fortune in their life together.

Funerals
Funerals, like weddings, vary greatly according to the religion, ethnic group, age, and position of the person who died. Nigerian funerals are costly events that often put a strain on the family of the deceased. Some ethnic groups have a protracted wake, generally at the home of the deceased. Many will hold a funeral service, followed days, weeks, or even months or years later by an elaborate memorial ceremony. Muslims in Nigeria follow the Islamic tradition of burial within twenty-four hours. A ceremony is then held three, seven, and/or forty days after death at the home of the deceased's family or at the mosque. Generally a funeral or memorial ceremony will be as large and elaborate an affair as the family can afford, including quantities of food and drink as well as memorial gifts for the guests.

Nigerians traditionally believe that a spirit never dies, and in general funerals or memorials celebrate a person's life rather than mourn their death. The Yoruba in particular celebrate the passing of an older person to the afterlife in a festive atmosphere, but the death of a young person may be minimally observed; sometimes parents may not even attend the funeral. This is not to say that they do not grieve, but it is considered a bad omen or "unnatural" to witness the funeral of someone so young—every parent prays that their children will bury them in old age and not vice versa.

OTHER TRADITIONS
Names

Names in all of Nigeria's cultures have a profound meaning that is felt to influence the life of the individual. Often names are related to circumstances surrounding the individual's birth, or articulate a hope for the future of the child, or form a link with an ancestor. Most Nigerians have more than one name—significant individuals, like the father, mother, and other close relatives, may each give the child a name that they will use exclusively. Christian children are given a baptismal name; Muslim Nigerians often have an Arabic or Persian name. As the child grows up, one name generally sticks and this is the one that the individual uses predominantly. The use of names is quite fluid: a person may choose to use any one of their given names in the course of their lives, or they may choose to adopt a Western name. Because names mean something in each language, a Nigerian will immediately know which tribe an individual belongs to upon hearing their name—a detail that, of course, escapes foreign visitors to the country.

EXAMPLES OF IGBO NAMES

Adachi: the daughter of God

Akachukwu: God's hand

Nwanyioma: beautiful lady

Ndidikanma: patience is best

EXAMPLES OF YORUBA NAMES

Jumoke: loved by all

Modupe: thanks

Foluke: in the hands of God

Oluwatobi: God is great, a first name usually shortened to Tobi

EXAMPLES OF HAUSA NAMES

Tanko: a boy born after successive girls

Labaran: a boy born in the month of Ramadan

Gagare: unconquerable

Afere: a girl born tiny

Chieftaincies and Titles

Each locality in Nigeria has a council of chiefs with a regional king: in the southwest chiefs are known as *oba*, in the southeast as *obi*, and in the north as emirs. Traditionally the Igbo live in small communities with an elected council rather than a chief, though chiefdoms are becoming more popular.

In most of the country, kingships are hereditary within the extended family: the "kingmakers," a group of well respected and influential men close to the court, will select an heir from among the members of the extended royal families. Some chiefdoms are hereditary, while others are earned through a demonstrated dedication to the community. An individual will be appointed for life as a chief to a specific council and for a specific role. Some of these roles are reserved for members of particular families in a community. In the current society, where wealth is a determinant of power and prestige, it is possible to buy a chieftaincy title. The title of chief brings with it prestige and power in local decision-making processes; it also brings the responsibility of looking out for the community, which often means providing financial support for community projects or to individuals in need.

The main source of income for kings and chiefs in the traditional power system came from their control over access to land and from the donations of their loyal subjects, as in feudal Europe. With the imposition of a Western democratic form of government, however, the traditional power structures lost their income base and their official power over their subjects. Today, traditional rulers are still important in maintaining the community's social cohesion and are the keepers of traditional rites, rituals, and cultural displays. Many are supported through financial contributions from state coffers. There is, therefore, a delicate balancing act between the formal state power structure and traditional power bases. Local politicians ignore the traditional leaders at their peril—they are very close to their constituent members and can make or break political careers.

National Youth Service

The National Youth Service Corps, started in 1973, requires all university and polytechnic graduates to perform one year of government service after graduation. The program provides work experience to graduates and helps fill public service posts, primarily in education. Graduates can arrange their own work placement or the government will provide them with a position, often in a public school. The program aims to provide individuals with work experience in a different part of the country from where they normally reside; in this way, national unity and interethnic understanding is stimulated. The program is broadly viewed as having laudable goals, though many feel that its implementation today is not as good as it used to be because of a lack of appropriate positions.

Sanitation Day

In Abuja and Lagos, road travel is banned
between 7:00 and 10:00 a.m. on the last Saturday
of every month for a municipal cleanup.
Citizens are expected to clean the environment
immediately outside their homes. The police
enforce the ban vigilantly, and anyone found
driving or wandering the streets (even jogging)
during these hours is fined.

Superstitions

Nigerian superstitions are related to the ancient
indigenous belief systems in which the spirit
world is present everywhere in the physical
world. Many beliefs, values, and superstitions
are expressed in sayings, either in native
languages or in Pidgin. Superstitions vary widely
across the country, but here are a few examples
that give a small taste of the rich world of subtle
associations and allusions in the culture:

- Discussions of death, wills, testaments, and
  so on are avoided because they are believed
  to beckon death.
- Nigerians don't like to be given an open
  bottled drink unless it has been opened in
  front of them, for fear that there may be
  juju or some other nasty thing that has
  been put inside.
- "*Chicken wey no dey hear word go hear word
  inside pepper soup*" ("The chicken who doesn't
  listen will understand once he's in the soup") –

meaning, a stubborn person will comply with all your demands/advice when he's in trouble.

- If you are setting out of your house on a journey and you trip, don't continue, as something bad may happen to you on your way or at your destination. You've just had a warning from your ancestors.
- If you sneeze, this means someone is talking about you.
- Don't whistle at night, because this encourages evil spirits or ghosts.
- If you hear your name called and you can't see who's calling, don't answer: it might be spirits calling you. If you answer, you might end up going to the underworld with them.

chapter four

MAKING FRIENDS

Nigerians bestow the appellation of "friend" on a very wide circle of acquaintances. Typically, friendships in Nigeria are based on shared difficulties, mutual traumas, experiences in common, and the ability to provide emotional, mental, or material comfort—that is, a solution to a problem. Friendships are made within a narrow band of age cohorts, but they can and do cross ethnic and religious lines—for instance, secondary school and university students are likely to make lifelong friends with people from other communities.

At a first meeting, Nigerians will probably be warm and friendly, perhaps even overwhelmingly so. You may immediately be greeted with "How are you, my friend?" However, many foreigners living in Nigeria find it difficult to get beyond the level of pleasant and easygoing acquaintanceship and into deeper friendship. For foreigners, there are certain constraints to making friends with Nigerians. First is the economic and power distance between Westerners and Nigerians. Many expatriates in Nigeria are in the country for work reasons and

are therefore almost certain to be in an income
bracket well beyond that of all but a very small
segment of Nigerian society. Students, NGO
workers, and other lower-paid individuals may
not face such a large gap but may still not be
perceived as being "equal." Second is the fact that
foreigners are, by definition, unknown. Nigerian
relationships are intricately related to one's family
and community background as well as one's
character and accomplishments; foreigners have
no verifiable background and are not easily placed
in the Nigerian social hierarchy, so it takes time to
establish trust. Finally, the strict social hierarchy
precludes any chance of friendships that cross
echelons—office juniors will be able to have
friendly relations with their equal colleagues, but
not with their bosses.

MEETING NIGERIANS

Where people meet will depend on familial
circumstances. Young, unmarried Nigerians in the
private sector or at university will lead social lives
not unlike their counterparts in the West. They
will probably tend to socialize outside the home,
going out to bars, restaurants, discos, and events,
more than at home, because they may still live
with their parents or in small accommodation. A
foreign visitor who is also single may eventually
get invited to such evenings if they indicate
their desire to go and once trust is established.

Older individuals who are married tend to have
a full plate of social responsibilities and do not

have as much time to socialize with colleagues. A casual, after-office dinner or drinks will be rare because most Nigerians have long drives home and children waiting; they therefore tend to leave the office immediately after work. Neither do Nigerians invite groups of friends or colleagues to Western-style sit-down dinners at their homes. You may get invited, probably as a lone guest, to the home of a colleague or business contact: such invitations are a true honor and should be treated as such. If you are invited out for a meal, it will most likely be in a restaurant and will probably be a large, formal, business-related event.

Beyond family networks, Nigerians mainly socialize through networks established at the church or mosque, or through community networks such as development organizations, work-related groups, or political structures. Some of the best ways to meet Nigerians are by joining the local golf club, becoming active in local charities like schools or orphanages, or visiting cultural sites such as museums or music centers.

INVITATIONS TO SPECIAL EVENTS

You may be invited to special events like a wedding, birthday, or funeral. These may or may not take place at home. Across the country, these events will most likely start at least an hour later than stated on the invitation and will last longer than you expect. It may be useful to ask a Nigerian what the realistic start time is and how long the event will last—better to be mentally prepared than to have to cancel other appointments during the ceremony.

If You Are Invited to a Wedding

For a wedding, you will receive an invitation that will tell you which part of the wedding you are invited to (such as the religious or traditional events). You will be invited either by someone from the bride's side of the family or the groom's. For most weddings this distinction is important as each side will be identified by the cloth that their outfits are made of—each family selects a different piece of material within a chosen color scheme. It can also happen that a group of people—school friends or work colleagues, for instance—will get together and choose their own material within that color scheme; they will then use a piece of the bride or groom's chosen cloth as a shawl or other accompaniment to identify their connection at the wedding.

If you are invited to a wedding, you will be given the opportunity to buy the cloth of the group to which you belong. If you are a woman you should buy the five yards (4.6 meters) of material from which a tailor can make you an outfit of your choice. Sometimes a separate print is used for a head tie that can also be used as a shawl (unless you have someone to tie it for you, the head piece can be rather complicated). Men can obtain material for a traditional suit (tunics of various lengths and trousers), but it is acceptable to buy enough for just a traditional cloth cap. You are not obliged to buy the material, but participating fully is fun. Your effort will also be appreciated by your hosts, not least because the family uses the proceeds from the sale of the material to help toward the (substantial) costs of the wedding.

If, for whatever reason, you do not wear traditional material to a wedding, men should go in a business suit with tie and women in a rather formal dress or skirt. Foreigners are excused many things by the very fact of being foreign, but being shabbily or informally dressed will not gain you any respect.

Bring a present to a wedding, particularly something for the kitchen like a set of glasses, a cooking pot, or a nice serving dish. Gift wrap your present. What you bring—that is, how much it costs—will depend on how well you know the happy couple.

At Muslim weddings, there may be separate events for men and women. Non-Muslim women are not expected to cover their heads in the north, and you are not expected to have a hat or other head gear. However, if you have a pretty shawl that goes with your outfit, bring it along to help you fit in.

If You Are Invited to a Funeral

You may receive a written invitation to a funeral, in which case it will be clear what type of funeral it is—which religion, whether it is a funeral or memorial service, and whether it will take place at the family home or in a separate location. Funerals and memorial services are very expensive, so offering an envelope with a contribution (perhaps the equivalent of 25 to 100 euros, or US$35 to US$145, depending on how well you knew the person or know a member of their family) will be very much appreciated.

More about Giving Gifts

There is not a big tradition around giving gifts in Nigeria beyond the examples given above, but if you are invited to someone's home or would like to give a gift to someone who has helped you out in a special way, or for any other reason, a small token will be well received. Household goods are always appreciated, as is food, such as fruit, nuts, or something typical from your home country. Note, however, that many Nigerians do not have a sweet tooth; candies, cookies, and chocolates will be gracefully received but may not be eaten by your hosts. Another possibility is a small gift for the children, particularly something that comes from your country. Remember that even in the south, many Nigerians are Muslim. For this reason, it is best to avoid offering alcoholic beverages or pork products as gifts unless you know for certain that no one in the family is Muslim. Furthermore, if you are a man and want to give something to a woman, be sure to mention that it comes from your wife, mother, or sister—it is bad form for you to give a woman something directly. Do wrap your gift—it may or may not be opened in front of you.

SOCIALIZING AND CONVERSATION

Nigerians greet each other in quite a formal manner. It would be unthinkable to call an older friend or acquaintance by their first name (though anyone younger will be called by their first name); instead, people will use a relationship title like auntie or uncle without the use of a first name, and sometimes even if there is no blood relationship. As a foreigner it would be awkward to start calling all older women auntie: it is best to address people by their title, or use Mr. or Mrs. and their last name until invited to use first names. (For more on this topic, see page 157.)

In the Yoruba culture a younger or less senior person will show their respect by lowering their head, kneeling down, or curtsying—or even, in some cases (such as when in front of a king), lying flat on the ground. This type of body language is seen as a sign of good upbringing and respect for traditions and social hierarchies.

Remember that Nigerian society is not egalitarian: if you are a high-level executive, your business contacts will not happily socialize with your driver around a table, and trying to organize such an event will cause offense. In fact, your driver or household staff will not want to be made to feel that they are your equal: their status comes from your status as a boss, and a good boss is someone who acts like one and takes care of their staff. Again, friendships are made between equals in terms of age and position within the social hierarchy.

Traditionally, an argument or disagreement between individuals is solved with the help of an intermediary. In this way, neither party loses face and the issue is resolved in a neutral environment. What this means for foreigners is that a Nigerian will not tell you if you have made a faux pas or have inadvertently insulted them. For example, Nigerians are very sensitive to condescension. If you have slighted someone, they will remain polite toward you, but you will not gain their trust or respect. If you realize that you have given offense, you can apologize directly. If you do not know what the cause of the problem is, ask another Nigerian—they will be able to tell you what the issue is and how to go about resolving it.

Topics of Conversation
Favorite topics of conversation are politics, corruption, and the daily hardships of life in

Nigeria; street sellers, students, office workers, and government employees all have strong opinions on "the state of Nigeria," and displays of strong emotions in public on these topics are common.

The topic of religion is highly sensitive. It is unwise to criticize any belief system. You may, however, be asked your religious views; while you may answer honestly, you risk shocking or offending a Nigerian if you reply that you are an atheist or nonreligious. In such a situation, you may want to temper your responses to this sensibility by answering that you are nonpracticing or prefer to keep such issues private. Furthermore, because most Nigerians are deeply religious, it is best never to use profanity, even in jest.

Another view that may be met with incomprehension is the idea that someone might not want to marry or to have children. In order to protect your own privacy but still satisfy your host's curiosity, you may want to answer something like "it just hasn't happened yet" or "still hoping . . ."

It is absolutely unacceptable for you, as a guest, to criticize the country—its politics, corruption, and so on—even if your hosts have launched into a long tirade themselves. Ask as many questions as you like, but try to avoid giving an opinion that appears to denigrate the country.

The topic of polygamous marriages is also sensitive because Nigerians realize that many foreigners frown on the practice. For this reason, it is better not to ask a man you do not know very well how many children he has. In some cultures it brings bad luck to count one's children; it also raises the issue of how many wives the man has. If you know him well and get onto the topic of children, you may ask if he has "many" children. He will then be free to say yes if this is the case, or to give you a specific number.

Humor

Nigerians are generally very good-humored and enjoy a good laugh. Their humor is in part a survival mechanism that attests to the attitude that it is better to laugh in the face of adversity than to give up and cry. Their wit can be biting, sarcastic, and often targeted at themselves.

Nigerians have a thing for acronyms, which are often a source of inspiration for pokes at their public services (or lack thereof). For example, the power company in Nigeria was known as the National Electric Power Authority (NEPA), which was nicknamed Never Expect Power Again. Hours after renaming it the Power Holding Company of Nigeria (PHCN) it was christened Please Have Candle Nearby or Problem Has Changed Name.

SOCIAL SENSITIVITIES

There is a taboo about using the left hand. Do not eat with it (for example, if you eat a sandwich or a bun with only one hand, use the right hand), and do not accept things or pass things on to others using only the left hand—use your right or both hands.

It is common and even good manners to compliment people in Nigeria, but when complimenting a member of the opposite sex, be careful not to be misunderstood. A man may compliment a woman on her latest hairdo, for example, but shouldn't linger on the topic. It is the same with people's belongings: exuberant praise may leave the person feeling obliged to give you what you covet.

If you are hosting a dinner for Nigerian guests, be sensitive to religious practice: Muslims, for instance, do not eat pork. Furthermore, always have juice or soft drinks for those who don't want alcohol. Finally, many Nigerians do not have a sweet tooth, so providing fruit with dessert is a safe option.

The topic of juju, black magic, witches, and charms (not to be confused with traditional healers, who are still widely used) is quite taboo. On the one hand, no one will ever admit to believing in these phenomena; Christianity and Islam hold such beliefs to be unreligious and outdated. On the other, the fear of the power of the spirit world is still strong among most Nigerians, even the well educated. In rural areas, tragic events are sometimes explained in terms of witchcraft, and the "witch" will be found in the form of an old woman or child. Exorcism, persecution, and sometimes death can be used to end the suspected spell.

A final word of caution: prostitution is outwardly frowned upon in Nigerian society but privately is a relatively common way for young women to get money to pay for their studies or to set themselves up in business. Married men are known to have "girlfriends" whom they support financially, in some cases setting them up in apartments. In places frequented by foreign men, women will linger in the hope of getting business for the night or of establishing a longer-term friendship. It is not uncommon for men to assume that these pretty women are just girls on a night out with friends, and to be surprised when they learn of their true intentions. Beware.

THE NIGERIANS AT HOME

There are large differences between rural and urban lifestyles in Nigeria and between the daily existence of those who live on less than US$1.25 a day, the middle class, and the wealthy elite. As a foreign visitor you may only ever visit the big cities and may never see how the majority of Nigerians live. Chances are that you will stay in an air-conditioned hotel and socialize with Nigerians who live in villas or nice apartments, but for the majority, home life is far more traditional than this modern image may have you believe.

HOUSING

It is roughly estimated that around one-third of the population lives in rural areas, one-third in small towns, and one-third in cities. In rural areas, the building materials and architecture of traditional homes vary throughout the country. In the Niger Delta, for instance, many homes are built on stilts over creeks or swamps and are made of wood and bamboo with a raffia frond roof. Traditional Igbo houses in the southeast are mud-covered bamboo frames protected with banana leaves. In the Hausa north, homes are built of conical mud "bricks" smoothed over with typically reddish earth and decorated with geometric designs. More modern homes in many (semi-)rural areas are built of dried mud bricks or cinder blocks.

In the countryside today, many Nigerians continue to live in family compounds. Men and women traditionally live in separate houses. Generally speaking, a compound consists of individual homes for each nuclear family unit, housing the head of the family and his wife (a separate hut for each wife if there is more than one), their married sons, their unmarried daughters, and all the grandchildren. Most rural homes have neither indoor plumbing nor electricity. In some areas people have access to boreholes (wells), but many must purchase water, especially safe drinking water, on the private market, typically delivered in plastic jerricans by someone pushing a wheelbarrow. Most make use of communal latrines.

In the towns, most people live in small, individual houses or compounds. Some have indoor plumbing. Every type of housing is to be found in the cities, from slums to high-rise apartments and luxurious homes with gardens. A generator is required to run electrical appliances like refrigerators and air-conditioning on a reliable basis, as power outages are frequent; diesel, however, is expensive and occasionally scarce. Publicly supplied water through the water mains is practically nonexistent, so most people have a cistern on top of their home or building that is filled by privately serviced water trucks, or they dig their own boreholes. In apartment buildings, residents may share the cost of a larger generator and cistern.

The majority of people in urban areas rent. Nigerian cities have been growing at a fast pace since independence, which means two things: firstly, that there is a lack of suitable

accommodation and overcrowding in many places, and secondly, that many city dwellers still have strong links to their region of origin. Many Nigerians return regularly to their "home town" to visit relatives and take care of their family responsibilities. Individuals who can afford it own a home in their family village or town.

Nigerian homes tend to be kept dark during the day, with thick drapes to keep out the sun's heat. Only the wealthy or foreign-educated tend to decorate their homes with, for example, paintings on the wall, partly because art has traditionally been linked to religious uses: masks and sculptures were designed for and used in traditional rituals, and because of their spiritual power they were not normally kept on display inside the home.

DAILY LIFE

For most Nigerians, the expression "*Nigeria na war o*" sums it up: life in Nigeria is war. Heat, heavy rains, the lack of electricity and basic social services such as garbage collection, public transportation, and water supply, as well as bad roads and poor and crowded housing conditions—all make daily life difficult for the vast majority of Nigerians.

Life is stressful, particularly in the cities. The cost of living for the average Nigerian is high— food is expensive because of a lack of investment in agriculture over the last fifty years; rent is also high, and exorbitant land prices mean that home ownership is limited to the lucky few. Many people live far from their workplace, which means high transportation costs and long workdays. Furthermore, there is no state-funded social security provision, so most Nigerians are keenly aware that their livelihoods depend on their own hard work, entrepreneurial spirit, and competitiveness in a market flooded with too many workers and too few jobs.

Many Nigerians often only eat one meal a day—bread and tea suffices for breakfast. In the countryside the main meal will be lunch, while in the cities it will be the evening meal. In both cases, the meal is most often taken together as a family and there will be enough food for unexpected guests. Except for those with generator-supported refrigerators Nigerians need to buy fresh food every day.

In terms of shopping for necessities, practically everything is available in Nigeria, but at a price. European, South African, North American, and Middle Eastern (mainly Lebanese) products such as clothing and household goods are available in boutiques and stores in the shopping malls of Lagos and Abuja. Large markets also provide all household and personal items, but at a lesser quality and price. Imported food products are available in small grocery stores and supermarkets; while produce may be more expensive than abroad, the variety is largely what foreigners are accustomed to.

For clothing, other than expensive imports, locals buy material from the markets and get tailors to make them clothes. They can also buy secondhand clothing and factory rejects in the market. Some new Nigerian designers have opened up exclusive shops, and several boutiques offer a selection of off-the-rack clothing for the home market.

FAMILY LIFE

The family is the basic unit from which all other aspects of daily life flow. To be outside a family unit is to be on the margins of society—a very precarious place indeed. The family in the Nigerian context is always the extended family. The title "father" indicates a biological father but also his brothers and any other significant men of his generation who are close to the family. When someone is introduced as "my sister," it could mean that the two have the same parents, have one common parent, or are related somehow within the extended family network—or not: two women addressing each other as "my sister" could simply be using a term of endearment, indicating a friendship that is valued as much as a family relationship. In general, however, there is not a lot of physical contact (like hugging) between family members; parents are unlikely to show overt affection to their children in public.

Most Nigerians spend much of their spare time with, or taking care of, members of their extended family. Making visits to, or receiving visits from, direct family members and in-laws is seen as a basic responsibility of every Nigerian, and is neglected at one's peril. While the extended family model is still the norm, Christianity has limited the number of polygamous marriages. Furthermore, the economic pressures of modern Nigeria, as well as higher levels of education, have tended to decrease family sizes, especially in the southern regions of the country.

Children
Across the country, children are seen as a blessing—the family network is the individual's social security system, to which children are future contributors. Children are primarily raised by their mothers, though the bringing up of children is seen as the responsibility of everyone in the family—families raise the children of those who cannot do so themselves, and all adults will reprimand children regardless of familial relations. In general, fathers are proud of their children, but are not often involved in raising them when they are young.

Children are loved but generally have little say in the decisions that affect their lives. They are expected to be respectful toward adults, hardworking, and mindful of their rights and responsibilities within the family network—their future successes will contribute to their family's honor and prestige. When women work outside the home, they often carry their children on their backs until they are old enough to be left with family members. Professional women in the cities will either be assisted by their family or will get a nanny, who will often be a relative from the home village. Children in wealthy households get the best education and are often sent to boarding schools in Nigeria, the UK, or the USA at some point between the ages of nine and fifteen.

Children begin to help around the house at a young age, and as they grow older they play an increasingly active role in family life. In rural areas this will likely be on the farm: boys herd the animals, girls fetch water and help around the house, and all children help with planting and harvesting. Later, many become apprentices in the family craft or trade, such as weaving, tailoring, cooking, hairdressing, or making pottery. In the cities and towns, children may supplement the family's income by working as street vendors or car washers, or helping in transporting goods. Poor rural families sometimes send a child to live with a richer relative in the city, where they are expected to help around the house in exchange for an education or training for other work opportunities.

Given the current job market, it is not a foregone conclusion that one's children will succeed in finding work and becoming independent. Even in families with the means to pay for a good education for their children, parents must deal with the fact that their (male) children may live with them for many years.

Young people who cannot find jobs also cannot afford to pay for their own housing. Marriage is expensive and many couples will live together, if need be in the paternal home, until they can afford the ceremony.

EDUCATION

Formal education in Nigeria is based on the British school system. Education has become very important to the upwardly mobile and internationally connected classes of Nigeria. Entry into better schools (federal secondary, state and federal universities, and private schools) is very competitive and expensive. Since independence the public system has expanded, but it has lost much of its ability to prepare children for a productive role in society. Problems include poor funding, shortage of qualified teachers, and a curriculum that does not reflect the needs of the economy. Private schools have sprung up to fill the gap in quantity and quality, many (charity and nonprofit schools) catering specifically to the country's poorest children. Many of the country's elite send their children abroad for their secondary education.

It is estimated that nationwide somewhere near 60 percent of school-age children attend primary school and just over one-third attend secondary school. These statistics hide wide discrepancies: the figures are far lower in the Muslim north than in the south, lower in rural areas than in urban centers, and far fewer girls attend school in the north than in the south.

Public primary schooling in Nigeria is theoretically free and compulsory, but uniforms, books, sandals, and transportation have to be paid for, and there are other hidden payments that are not called fees but are nonetheless required contributions. Primary school goes from the ages of six to eleven, and secondary school from twelve to seventeen. All classes, except in the Koranic schools, are taught in English. A native language is also taught. Because of the inadequate funding of schools through official channels, there is a lot of parental and community involvement in primary schools. Groups of concerned parents contribute to the schools through construction and maintenance projects, and fund-raising for furniture, books, and other school materials.

At the secondary level there are state as well as federal schools, and competition is fierce to get into the better ones. There are also private secondary schools, which vary in quality and fees charged. There are currently thirteen federal and fourteen state-owned colleges and universities in Nigeria, but it is generally recognized that the quality of the degrees has diminished over the years, and that too many courses are not suited to the job market. In general, there are too few science degrees, and those that exist stress theory over practical application of knowledge or experience.

There are many extremely well educated Nigerians who have studied in the Oxfords and

Harvards of Europe and North America. In fact, Nigerians tend to do well overseas: of all the foreign communities living in London, Nigerians are the second-highest average wage earners, after Americans. With the economic crisis in Europe and North America, many of these well-educated, successful individuals are returning to their homeland and filling top jobs in the private and public sectors. Accustomed to a Western lifestyle, they are becoming an important pressure group for development and change in Nigeria. Their financial and personal investments in their country are already having a beneficial impact.

NIGERIAN YOUTH

As we've seen, in Nigeria approximately one-third of all secondary school-age children go to school. Not surprisingly, urban youth are more likely to be in school than their rural counterparts, more children are in school in the south than in the north, and the wealthier the parents, the more likely it is that their children will be in school. Northern rural girls are the least likely to be in school.

There are, therefore, huge differences in the experience of teenage years among Nigeria's young people. Those children who a get a top education and have good job prospects after graduating are on a par with internationally educated young people around the world. In Nigeria, those not in schools or in under-performing schools have far bleaker prospects. An urban phenomenon known as "area boys" is the Nigerian version of youth gangs. They are notorious for petty crimes and neighborhood extortion rackets. Nigeria's birthrate for teenage girls is one of the highest in the world. In the north, where polygamous marriages are more common, girls tend to marry younger than in the south. Many children, therefore, experience a truncated youth, moving quickly into the adult world well before their eighteenth birthdays.

There are also Nigerian adolescents whose lives are similar to those of Western teenagers, however: they go to school and have to contend with attentive parents who want them to succeed. Some have access to sports and other activities, but mainly they focus on their academic work. They are plugged into Nigerian and international pop music and TV, and go out with friends on weekends or visit each other at home. Arguably the most important difference between Western and Nigerian teens is that,  whether rich or poor, Nigerian teenagers are far more aware of just how hard they need to work to succeed. They will, therefore, tend to lead a somewhat less carefree adolescence than their Western peers. This does not mean they are less happy, just that they are more aware, at a younger age, that their future success in life depends, at least in part, on how hard they themselves work at achieving success.

TIME OUT

Apart from public holidays and festivals, the vast majority of Nigerians have very little leisure time. They work long days and spend hours in the traffic getting home, and many work a six-day week. The little time they do have free is mainly spent with their extended family or attending to religious practices or social obligations.

Evenings or Sunday afternoons may be spent with friends at a bar or local meeting place, watching television or Nigerian DVDs. For the middle class, the wealthy, and foreign visitors or residents, the large cities such as Lagos and Abuja provide ample opportunities for leisure activities: cinemas, bowling alleys, parks, the beach (in Lagos), swimming pools, golf, fitness clubs, tennis, shopping, bars and restaurants, art galleries—there is more than enough to choose from.

FOOD AND DRINK

As a rule, Nigerian families have the evening meal together. Home-cooked meals are the ideal, but busy lives mean that ready-made meals are often bought from stalls offering a variety of local dishes that are made and served hot to be eaten on the spot or as takeout. There are fast-food restaurants serving local dishes, often chicken and spicy rice varieties, or continental dishes such as pizza or sandwiches. Kentucky Fried Chicken has opened in Lagos. All the major cities in Nigeria have a wide variety of restaurants, including those that serve European, Asian, and Lebanese cuisine. Eating in Western-style restaurants is not cheap, but the quality is generally good. In general, eating out in restaurants will be saved for special occasions.

Nigerian food is similar to that found in the rest of West Africa. It is based on staples such as sweet potatoes and plantain; yam and cassava are pounded and mixed with water to make a mashed potato-like paste in the south, and sorghum is used for a thick porridge in the north. These are accompanied by spicy (quite hot for many Western palates) vegetable-based stews with bits of meat (beef, chicken, or goat) or

(dried) fish added. One dish worth trying is pepper soup—hotel restaurants often serve a nice pepper soup of chicken or fish and will make it less spicy for Western tastes. Other local favorites are *suya* (spicy barbecued beef on sticks) and grilled corn on the cob, both of which can be found at street stalls as well as in many restaurants. In the north, *kilishi* (spiced dried meat) is a specialty. Across the country, *egusi* soup, a stew of meat, dried fish, and melon seeds, is popular. Prawns (particularly large and tasty) and fresh fish are abundant on the coast.

TIPPING

Tips for services—from the bellhop, the man who helps you park, the man who packs your groceries, and so on—are expected, though not compulsory. They need not be a large sum. Remember, while there are some very rich Nigerians, the majority live on very low salaries. You should see this in the context of the patronage system that flavors all of Nigeria's social relationships: you are perceived as being a rich white person, which means that you are worthy of respect and assistance in return for tips. This is the client-patron system. Sometimes, a 10 percent service charge is put on hotel and restaurant bills, though you may still want to leave the waiter a small something. If there is no service change, a 10 percent tip is very respectable.

Smoking

About 12 percent of the population smokes—more men than women and more (many more) in the north than in the south. Youth, however, are smoking more, which is partially an image thing—it is Western and cool. The Nigerian National Tobacco Control Bill prohibited smoking in public places and made it illegal to sell to minors under the age of eighteen. Generally the attitude to smoking is lenient, but there is little smoking in restaurants in the south. As anywhere in the world, you may want to ask the people you are with if they mind you smoking, and even if they say that they do not, consider going outside.

Drinking

The main locally produced alcoholic drinks are palm wine and gin. Beer is locally produced by foreign companies such as Heineken (with a local favorite called Star) and Guinness. These companies also produce a line of popular malt drinks that are dark and frothy and not unlike nonalcoholic beer. Wine and spirits from around the world are available in stores and restaurants in the cities, as is locally produced gin. In this highly religious country where family and community still exert pressure on individual behavior, alcoholism and drug abuse exist, but are not a widespread problem. Paradoxically, alcoholism is more of a problem in the Islamic north than in the south.

As much as 70 percent of the population is estimated not to drink at all, and in restaurants it will be extremely rare to see a drunken person. It is not advisable to get drunk in public—you won't get any brownie points for it.

Drug abuse

Drug abuse is not (yet) a major problem in the country, though it is estimated that around 10 percent of the population use cannabis at some time in their lives. The larger drug abuse problems exist in the northern region of the country. Possession, use of, or trafficking in illegal drugs is a serious offense and can result in lengthy prison sentences and heavy fines.

SPORTS

Nigeria is a football (soccer) nation— millions of Nigerians avidly follow national and European competitions. Bets can be placed in makeshift roadside stands, where the next games are announced on chalkboards. Nigeria has twenty teams competing in its Professional League, and its national team competes in international competitions such as the World Cup and the Olympics. There are more than 360 Nigerian players who play on European and South American teams. Soccer leagues for children also exist, and informal games start up everywhere in the country in any area large enough for a game. Many Nigerian children dream of becoming stars.

Nigeria is also competitive internationally in weight lifting, boxing, and track and field. Among the Yoruba, traditional wrestling is an ancient and popular sport. Sports such as swimming, tennis, table tennis, handball, basketball, squash, cricket, judo, field hockey, weight lifting, and wrestling are supported by the government, corporate bodies, and individuals.

Polo is very popular among Nigeria's elite, blending the northern expertise and tradition with horses with the imported British game. There are around eleven polo clubs in Nigeria, including those in Abuja, Lagos, Port Harcourt, and Katsina. National and international competitions are held regularly.

Finally, there are golf courses in Abuja and Lagos, and many clubs, compounds, and hotels are equipped with facilities for swimming, tennis, squash, fitness, and aerobics.

THE ARTS

Nigeria is full of talent, be it in music, literature, or the fine arts, and there are many top and internationally renowned artists making the Nigerian cultural scene "the place to be" on the continent.

Music

In the 1960s, new musical styles such as highlife (from Ghana) and juju blended African folk music with Western jazz and blues and Latin American influences. However, it is Fela Anikulapo Kuti (1938–70) who created a Nigerian form of Afrobeat that in its turn influenced music around the world. Fela Kuti is Nigeria's most famous musician, honored today through the Broadway musical *Fela!*. Nationally he is remembered not only for his contribution to Nigerian music, but also, through his lyrics, as a political activist who stood up to Nigeria's military dictators. Writing mostly in Pidgin English, he expressed people's frustrations over the harshness of their daily lives and the politics that got them there.

Today, Nigeria continues to produce great musicians. Fela's son Femi Kuti has twice been nominated for a Grammy Award for his Afrobeat sound. Asa, a young Yoruba singer-songwriter, has become very popular in Nigeria and Europe with her folksy songs and politically motivated lyrics. Dr. Segun Akinlolu won the 2004 Galaxie Rising Stars Award for folk music in Ontario, Canada. But the most popular music with young people today is Nigerian hip-hop, with acts like P-Square, D-Banj, Plantashion Boyz, Remedies, Styl-plus, Zakky, and Sunny Nneji.

In Lagos, the Musical Society of Nigeria, based at the Muson Centre, aims to promote the enjoyment and performance of classical music by running an award-winning school of music and hosting a full program of performances throughout the year.

Film

Generally known as Nollywood, the Nigerian film industry is estimated to produce around one to two thousand movies a year. Nollywood films are more popular in Africa than Hollywood or Bollywood films, and are popular with the Nigerian and African diaspora around the world. The industry employs thousands of people and generates between US$200 and 300 million per year. The films are produced for the home CD market since there are very few cinemas in the country. An average film sells around 50,000 copies. The discs sell for about US$2 each, which makes them affordable for most Nigerians.

The average budget for a movie is about US$10,000. Their low technical quality and the fact that many use liberal amounts of Pidgin English have limited their appeal. The themes of the films cover issues that are important to Nigerians today, including family issues, changing values, love, moral dilemmas facing modern Africans such as corruption and abuse of power, AIDS, and women's rights. In terms of religion, some promote either the Christian or the Islamic faith; while some movies are overtly evangelical, others address issues of religious diversity such as interfaith marriage. Watching Nigerian movies is a good way of keeping abreast with what the majority of Nigerians are talking about.

Visual Art

Traditionally, art in Nigeria was an integral part of the spiritual life of the community. This can be seen in the wooden and bronze sculptures, masks, and even doors of exquisite artistry that the country has produced. Today they are collected by foreigners and museums around the world.

The concept of art as an independent aesthetic medium really began in the early twentieth century, when universities, funded through British programs, trained a new brand of Nigerian artist. At this point, traditional art became associated with craft, and a new wave of contemporary art began. This included painting, modern sculpture, engraving and photography, installations, and video art. Today there is a vigorous fine art scene despite the fact that there is little public funding for artists. The National Council for Arts and Culture and the National Gallery of Art, two publicly funded institutions, and the international Goethe Institute and the French Cultural Centre, have all provided support for the development of Nigerian art. More recently, the African Artists' Foundation (a private Nigerian organization) and many private galleries have provided venues for Nigeria's artists to exhibit their work, both within the country and internationally. The art scene is mainly found in Lagos, where there are weekly exhibitions, talks, and other events featuring painting and sculpture as well as fashion, photography, and installations.

Nigerian painters are recognized worldwide. Nationally the impact of the art is limited to the urban elite, though individual artists do make an effort to reach out to the mass of the people, and it is a source of great national pride to know that these artists are successful abroad.

Fine art in Nigeria tends to be secular, reflecting themes such as the difficulty of everyday life and the power, beauty, and resilience of Nigeria's people. Much of the work is abstract, using intense, vibrant colors that express a strong sense of identity and self-confidence. In visiting art galleries or exhibits, one gets a strong sense of the Nigerians' irrepressibly positive attitude toward life. Many contemporary Nigerian artists have works in important museum collections around the world, and several have recently done well in auctions at Christie's and Sotheby's.

Literature

It is estimated that around 68 percent of all Nigerians are literate. The market for Nigerian and foreign literature is very small as the number of people who read for pleasure is small. The best Nigerian authors, therefore, draw on their experiences at home but are aware that they need to make their books accessible to foreign audiences, including the large numbers of Nigerians and other Africans overseas. Nigeria has long been recognized for its

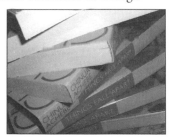

literary talent, which stems from a long-established art of storytelling. The list of internationally recognized writers includes Chinua Achebe, Wole Soyinka, Chimamanda Ngosi Adichie, Helon Habila, Sefi Atta, and Adaobi Tricia Nwaubani.

SHOPPING FOR PLEASURE

Nigeria is primarily known for its arts and crafts, materials, and, increasingly, locally designed clothing and accessories. These products are all found primarily in specialized boutiques and art galleries, as well as the outdoor markets around town.

Markets

There are some wonderful markets in Nigeria selling handicrafts and local produce. Fruit and vegetable markets are generally small and scattered around the city. Craftworks, such as old and modern wooden carvings and new Benin bronzes, are available in the markets, as are articles made from woven grass, sculptures, leatherwork, calabashes, pottery, and bead- and metalwork. Beautiful Nigerian and West African materials are also widely available. There are many tradesmen who sell tablecloths, aprons, and towels made from local tie-dye batiks. Some markets specialize in specific products: the camel markets of northern Nigeria, the material markets of Abeokuta, and the craft market of Lagos are good examples.

Bargaining

Many visitors to Nigeria who are not accustomed
to bargaining can feel that they are being taken
advantage of, but it helps to bear in mind that in
the West the price of goods includes a large
markup that customers neither see nor have any
control over. Negotiating for your purchases in
Nigeria is about finding "fair" value—for instance,
it is considered normal to get a slightly higher
price from a foreigner, who can afford to pay
more, than from a poor Nigerian. The seller has a
bottom price, under which they have calculated
that they will lose money, and they will try to get
as much of a profit as possible. As a buyer, how
much you are willing to pay depends on how
much you value that item—how much you want
it, how easy it is to get elsewhere, and what you
feel is a "fair" profit for the seller.

In shops and boutiques, where prices are
clearly labeled, there is generally no bargaining,
though if you feel like asking politely you may be

given a discount. Bargaining in markets is the norm and is a serious though good-natured process. Generally you can offer under half the price that is quoted and try to stay as close to that as possible. If you pick up a product, the seller will assume that you are seriously in the market for it. If you walk away from a negotiation and they come back to you with another offer, you will be seen as very impolite if you don't take it. It is wise to ask people before you go to the market what the going rate is for products you want to buy—this will help you gauge how hard you need to bargain. Alternatively, you could bring along an experienced friend if one is available.

The concept of window-shopping is alien to Nigerians: they shop because they need something. If you spend hours wandering around the market and buy nothing, people will assume that you are stealing ideas in order to make your own products and make money from other people's ideas. While this may seem ludicrous to foreigners, you may notice sellers becoming aggressive and unfriendly if you are not buying.

TOURISM

Nigeria is not yet geared toward tourism—even getting a tourist visa is nigh impossible without a local host. Nigerians themselves travel throughout their country, but not often for leisure—they visit family or go on business trips. The country has not yet developed a tourism mentality or infrastructure. This does not mean that there is nothing to see, however. Those who live here for longer periods have the opportunity to visit some of Nigeria's cultural and natural gems and to see the festivals that can otherwise only be viewed in coffee-table books or online.

One note of caution: when traveling around Nigeria, especially in the cities, be very careful when taking photographs. Ask first, and if people refuse, do not insist by trying to take a photo secretly. Some people may pose proudly, while others feel very strongly that they are being treated like animals in a zoo. Also, if you take pictures of someone performing their craft (such as a textile designer), they may worry that you intend to steal their design or process secrets. Furthermore, taking pictures in what are considered politically sensitive places, such as airports and near military bases, can get you in a lot of trouble.

One group that makes Nigeria's limited tourism possible is the Nigerian Field Society, a national organization that depends entirely on local interest and volunteer commitment. It is devoted to the study of all aspects of culture and the environmental sciences in Nigeria, including fauna and flora, history, archaeology, geology, legends and customs, arts and crafts, sports and other pastimes. It promotes natural conservation and cultural preservation as well as encouraging tourism in Nigeria. Its members, most of whom are Nigerian, organize visits to many of Nigeria's "highlights." Here are a few.

Obudu Mountain Resort in Cross River State

A former cattle ranch in the 1950s, this resort is now supported by the state's governor and is one of Nigeria's most favored destinations. A cable car system brings guests from the resort entrance at the bottom of the mountain to the ranch on the hilltop, where a temperate climate, breathtaking views, pleasant accommodation, and good restaurants make this a wonderful retreat.

Yankari National Park and Wikki warm spring in Bauchi State

Now managed by Buachi state government, Yankari National Park offers chalet facilities, restaurants, game drives (mainly smaller animals such as antelope), and dips in the beautiful natural springs, making it well worth a visit.

The beaches of Lagos

Many Nigerians and foreigners rent huts on the beaches both east (reached only by boat) and west (reached by car) of Lagos. These provide a lovely tropical setting for spending a quiet and relaxing day away from the bustle of the city.

Kano City in Kano State

Kano, the oldest city in West Africa, is still a
trading center—in the fascinating Kurmi Market
you can find woven materials, indigo-dyed cloth,
and leatherwork. The dye pits, the Grand Mosque,
the Emir's Palace, and the Gidan Makama
Museum all make a visit to this ancient, vibrant
Islamic city worthwhile.

Oshogbo Sacred Grove in Ogun State

In earlier times, each Yoruba village had its sacred
grove, an area of unspoiled forest where the gods

were worshipped. The Oshogbo forest was
rescued from its demise (it is the last known grove
of its kind) by the late Austrian artist and Yoruba
priestess, Susanne Wenger. She not only restored
ancient shrines but also began the new sacred art
movement, which stimulated Nigerian artists to
express their connection to the spirit world
through works of art. The groves are now a
unique collection of spiritual art that has been
added to UNESCO's list of World Heritage sites.
To priests, priestesses, devotees, and visitors from
Nigeria and around the world, the Oshogbo
Sacred Grove is now an important center of
Yoruba religious practice and spiritual expression.

The city of Calabar

Calabar boasts a carnival, a museum, and two primate protection centers. The festival was initiated in 2004 as a means of showcasing and preserving the Cross River State's cultural heritage. A huge street party and costume parade that takes place every December 26 and 27 includes concerts, soccer tournaments, art and cultural exhibitions, and a beauty pageant. The museum, showcasing the region's history, is probably the best museum in Nigeria. The Calabar Drill Monkey Ranch is a well run rehabilitation and captive breeding center for drills and chimpanzees, while the Cercopan Primate Sanctuary is a nonprofit NGO that provides sanctuary to guenons and mangabeys and stimulates primate protection through rain forest conservation, education, and research.

chapter seven

TRAVEL, HEALTH, & SAFETY

Nigeria is no more dangerous for visitors than most other African or Latin American countries. Foreign visitors are most likely to be driven around in private four-wheel drives or to fly. The country's infrastructure and public transportation are not up to par, and for most Nigerians, who do not own cars, traveling around the country is difficult, time-consuming, and uncomfortable.

ARRIVING IN NIGERIA

To enter Nigeria you need a passport valid for at least six months and a visa, as well as a yellow-fever stamp in your vaccination booklet. Procedures at the airports in Abuja and Lagos are normal. There are occasional delays due to power outages, but the formalities of passport control and collecting your luggage should go smoothly.

There is no public transportation from the airport into the city. You will need to be met at the airport either by someone you know or a representative of the company you are visiting, or by prearranged transportation provided by the hotel at which you will be staying. Taxis are available outside all airports and are probably safe in Abuja and Kano. In Lagos and especially in Port Harcourt, visitors are advised to arrange transportation to their destination before their arrival at the airport. Make sure that the greeter or driver can properly identify themselves, as bogus representatives have been known to be a problem. Outside the airports there are many baggage handlers hoping to help you push your cart for a tip. If you choose to use one, be sure they don't pull a fast one and run off with your luggage.

DRIVING

Generally, foreign visitors do not drive themselves in Nigeria. Some long-term foreign residents and many Nigerians do drive around, particularly on weekends— they are accustomed to driving conditions and know the roads and where to go. They will also be attuned to local security issues. However, as a short-term or first-time visitor, it's best to arrange for a good-quality car (four-wheel drives are the best choice) and an experienced and reliable driver. Alternatively, cars can be rented at the airport or major hotels: Hertz, Avis, and Europcar offer chauffer-driven cars for hire. Also, there are private drivers who have experience and good reputations with hotels and companies. Wear your seat belt—this rule is strictly enforced across the country.

Driving, or rather, being driven, is a sport of its own in Nigeria. While traffic drives on the right,

signposting is not optimal and maps, while
available, are not always up to date—getting lost is a
real possibility. Furthermore, driving conditions are
complicated by the sheer number of cars, trucks,
and other forms of transportation on the roads, the
poor automotive maintenance standards that mean
vehicles often break down in traffic, and
unpredictable driving standards (there tends to be
a competitive, "me-first" approach to driving in
which drivers concentrate on what is ahead without
looking in their rearview mirrors). Heavy rains
can also disrupt the flow of traffic on the roads.

In Abuja and Lagos, daytime car travel is
generally quite safe, though you may be stopped
by police or military checkpoints. Generally they
are hoping for a "dash" (a "tip"), or to find
something wrong with your papers that will
enable them to fine you. Nigerians feel that this
sort of petty corruption should be resisted,
though their daily lives are made more difficult
by this principled stance. Foreigners should resist
giving any money at all—by remaining calm,
smiling, and asking after the health of the officer

you will probably be waved on with a resigned look. If your car breaks down or is involved in an accident, do not get involved. Foreigners are seen as a source of cash. Stay quietly in the car and let your driver do the talking. Keep your windows shut and doors locked when driving.

STREET HAWKERS

As you drive through the streets of the major cities you will see young men laden with goods dangerously navigating the traffic during "go-slows" (traffic jams), running alongside a car as the driver rolls down the window to pass a few naira. These street vendors sell anything, from cell phone credit to colorful toilet seats; from handy connectors for charging any kind of phone in your car to do-it-yourself books, cheap plastic toys, and large, framed photographs of outdoor scenes in foreign countries; from soft drinks and cold water to fresh fruit, dried plantain chips, and "mealies" (dough with processed meat filling).

Ostensibly for road safety reasons, the government regularly sweeps the streets clean of these entrepreneurs, but for the unemployed and ambitious Nigerian, street trade is an easy and attractive way to earn some money. Each salesman will try to make eye contact to entice you with his wares. A friendly smile and shake of the head will earn you a bright smile in return before he moves on to the next car.

GETTING AROUND TOWN

There are several forms of "public" transportation in Nigeria, all of which are offered through private companies. Note that it is not common for expatriates to use public transportation, and no Nigerian who can afford a car would do so either. However, if you do, you will attract open and friendly curiosity, and will probably have a very pleasant, if not quiet, experience.

The *okada* is a motorcycle that takes one passenger on the seat behind the driver. They are very popular with Nigerians because they are cheap and offer a quick door-to-door service. State governments are trying to control or limit their use, however, mainly because of the number of traffic accidents they are involved in.

Small three-wheeled *tuk-tuks* known locally as *keke marwas* (yellow) and *keke napep* (green) take up to four passengers. They are slightly cheaper than *okadas*, but there are few of them.

Taxis in Nigeria are generally yellow with a black stripe. In Lagos there are new, red taxis that are meter operated. Taxis are generally used like buses—more than one client uses them at a time to go to the same general area. You can hire them on your own, but you will pay more for the ride.

There are mainly two types of buses in Nigerian cities: the *molue*, a yellow commercial bus that has longer routes and takes up to fifty passengers, and the *danfo*, a (mainly white) minibus that seats up to eighteen passengers and does both long and shorter routes. A tout, generally a young man, calls out the route and collects the bus fare, which tends to fluctuate with road conditions, gasoline scarcity, and demand. In Lagos State, a private bus system has begun with comfortable buses. These are a bit more expensive, and again, there are not enough of them to meet demand.

For all of the above, be sure to agree on a price before you start your journey because fares will vary depending on your destination, the number of passengers, and the whim of the driver or tout.

TRAVEL BETWEEN CITIES

By road: There are around 125,000 miles (200,000 km) of roads in Nigeria, though only a fraction are paved and maintained. The death toll on the roads is a common complaint in the news, and police and army roadblocks further hamper conditions. Nonetheless, road travel is possible with high-quality vehicles, recommended and

experienced drivers, and a realistic estimation of how long it will take you to get where you are going. There are also comfortable, air-conditioned buses that cover certain intercity, cross-state, and international bus routes (such as from Lagos to the border of Benin). Prices are reasonable and the service is good and safe, though delays during these journeys remain an issue.

By air: There are international airports in Lagos, Abuja, Kano, and Port Harcourt, and national airports in Calabar, Enugu, Jos, Kaduna, Sokota, Yola, and Maiduguri. Air travel is very busy, and it is advised to book tickets in advance. Safety has improved lately, though flight delays occur regularly. All domestic airlines have Web sites with flight information, prices, and so on.

WHERE TO STAY
There are large international hotels and smaller boutique hotels in Nigerian cities that are up to

international standards. In smaller towns there are often guesthouses run privately or by a company for its visiting staff or guests. Generally, you need to pay a deposit of up to twice the room rate upon arrival; your final bill will probably include the room rate, 5 percent VAT, and 10 percent service charge. There may also be an extra "fee," so check before what the total price will be before checking in. Most hotels charge in Nigerian naira, though dollars may be accepted in the larger establishments.

Prebooking is highly recommended, but do not give your credit card details to anyone—there is a serious risk of fraud. If you need to pay a deposit to make a booking, it is best to give cash (maybe someone can arrange this for you if you are not in the country). Nearly all hotels have their own generator to provide power during the frequent power outages—check, however, whether they keep the generator going at night or you will not have air-conditioning. Opening windows can be risky unless you have a mosquito net because of the prevalence of malaria.

Money
Nigerian currency is called naira (1 naira = 100 kobo). Notes come in denominations of 5, 10, 20, 50, 100, 200, 500, and 1,000 notes. Payment is always in naira.

It is advised not to use credit cards in Nigeria because of the potential for fraud. ATM machines and card payment facilities in shops and restaurants do exist and are on the increase, but if you can avoid using them, do so. Major hotels are generally OK. Inexplicably, it is difficult to exchange money at banks in Nigeria. There are Travelex offices at the airports and large hotels may be able to oblige you (US dollars are the best bet), though they will probably guide you to the black market sellers, who are tolerated.

HEALTH

Most travelers to Nigeria will encounter few major health risks, but certain precautions are necessary. Yellow fever is common in Nigeria, and you will be asked to show proof at the airport that you have had the yellow fever vaccination. Schistosomiasis (bilharzia), polio, and hepatitis A, B, and E occur in Nigeria, as do outbreaks of cholera. The prevalence of HIV is estimated at between 3 and 5 percent of the adult population—the second-highest rate in Africa. The biggest risk facing foreign guests, however, is malaria, which is common throughout the country, particularly the dangerous falciparum strain, which is resistant to chloroquine.

Use mosquito repellent, take malaria tablets, and wear long, light-colored clothing if you are outside at dusk or in the evening.

Do not drink the tap water—use bottled water or boil the water first. As in many tropical countries, be careful about the food you eat, especially before you become accustomed to it. Quality restaurants can generally be trusted to serve clean and fresh food, but be wary of eating salad and raw vegetables or fruit unless peeled. Make sure that meat and fish is well cooked and served hot.

There are state-provided health care facilities across the country, though they are of a low standard and experience shortages of drugs, equipment, electricity, and qualified personnel. In the cities there are reasonable hospitals; in rural areas people are most likely to mix public health provision with traditional medicine. For foreigners, good private clinics are available in all the main cities. There are also many excellent specialists who run private practices. Make sure you have adequate medical insurance.

ENVIRONMENTAL ISSUES

Apart from the need to get adjusted to the heat, the foreign visitor will not feel many effects of the environmental issues facing Nigeria. In the countryside problems include soil degradation, rapid deforestation, and desertification. In the cities, a lack of public services in waste management and water usage causes severe environmental degradation. The lack of sewage facilities, for instance, poses serious threats to health and is the leading cause of problems such as diarrhea and the spread of waterborne diseases. Trash, especially plastic, is a major pollutant in all urban areas. In the Niger Delta, soil and water pollution has been caused primarily by illegal tapping of oil (called bunkering), and in Zamfara

State, in the north, small-scale gold mining has contaminated the soil and water supply, with high concentrations of lead killing hundreds of children in neighboring villages.

SAFETY

There are a few security issues that all foreign visitors and returning Nigerians should be aware of. The big one relates to the Delta area, including the cities of Port Harcourt and Warri. This is the oil-producing area, where long-standing tensions exist between the peoples of the region, who feel shortchanged in the distribution of national wealth, and the federal government and oil companies. In recent years, local militants and criminal gangs have taken to kidnappings for financial gain. Particularly targeted are Nigerian workers in the oil industry and their families, including their children, even very small children. The security situation in the region is such that it is advised to travel, even by day, in a convoy of cars, and to avoid traveling at night at all.

Petty theft, armed robbery, carjacking, and politically or financially motivated kidnappings in other areas are not unheard of, including in Lagos and Abuja. The vast majority of Nigerians are upright, kind, and hospitable people, but as 70 percent of the population lives below the international poverty line, it is inevitable that some individuals will turn to crime for a living. Whether in a hotel, guesthouse, or private home, make sure you keep your valuables safe and your keys with you at all times. People are advised to avoid traveling late at night, except in groups. Avoid carrying large amounts of cash and do not wear valuable watches, jewelry, or items of sentimental value.

Furthermore, in the northern and middle-belt regions there are interethnic and interreligious tensions that smolder under the surface and can flare at any moment, and since the car bombings in Abuja during the celebrations of Nigeria's fiftieth anniversary of independence in 2010, there is a higher risk of terrorist activity across the country. However, these types of threats are limited to very small areas—and you can be at the wrong place at the wrong time anywhere in the world. Generally, northerners are not aggressive, and moving about feels very safe. Your hosts will know which areas to avoid and when.

Having said all of this, there is a very large community of expatriates who live in Nigeria quite happily. The safety precautions they follow vary immensely: some of the large multinationals insist that their staff have armed escort to certain parts of town, while those who own or manage small companies drive themselves everywhere. Houses, apartment complexes, and hotels are surrounded by walls and guarded twenty-four hours a day. People jog in the neighborhood of Ikoyi in Lagos and walk without hassle in the busy markets in many cities across the country.

chapter eight

BUSINESS BRIEFING

> *"No Nigerian arrangement is permanent unless that which has been arrived at by negotiated compromise."*
> How to be a Nigerian *by Peter Enahoro*

THE BUSINESS CULTURE

Nigerians are sophisticated businesspeople. They are intelligent, natural entrepreneurs, known for their perseverance and ingenuity. In general, Nigerians are hardworking and eager to learn. They also tend to be confident about their own abilities—many of those you'll meet are at the top

of their profession in the Nigerian context though some may overestimate their talents in comparison to the international labor pool.

The Nigerian business environment is deeply influenced by culture, relationships, and vested interests. In order to be successful, foreigners need to develop an understanding of, and respect for, the culture of their hosts.

What's so Difficult about Business in Nigeria?

A 2009 report by the International Bank for Reconstruction and Development ranks Nigeria 125th out of 183 economies in terms of "ease of doing business." There are several reasons for this. First, government bureaucracy is neither transparent nor efficient. Inconsistencies between federal and state regulations can lead to double taxation, contradictory requirements, and lengthy procedures. Also, legal and regulatory frameworks are weak: while contracts are generally recognized and respected, if a dispute arises, redress can be a lengthy, costly procedure. As a foreigner, you are at a distinct disadvantage in a country where the legal system can still be influenced by long-established local and national networks. Finally, trade unions are very powerful in the country and should be handled with care. In such an environment, the importance of establishing and maintaining relations based on trust and mutual respect is vital.

And then there is the issue of corruption. Do not assume that everyone is corrupt—they are not. Many in government and in the private sector are fighting corruption seriously. You can and should do business without offering bribes or giving in to indications that bribes are desired. This means that doing business in Nigeria may take longer than in other parts of the world.

The Importance of Relationships

Nigeria can be described as a relationship-oriented culture. This means that who you know is important, but also that the process of developing the relationship is as important as the business at hand: the context is as important as the content. In other words, it is necessary to take the time to get to know the person you are dealing with and to show them genuine respect. Trying to rush a deal or force a decision is bad manners and will not gain you any friends or respect.

Few people in any organization have the power to make decisions. You must therefore identify who the key person is and then gain access to them. This can be difficult because such people tend to be very busy and highly in demand. People in middle management should not be ignored entirely, however; they may be in a position to influence or gain the ear of the decision makers.

Even though officially illegal, favoritism and nepotism are still common practices. This flows naturally from the importance of family and "clan" in Nigerian culture. There is a very strong expectation placed on individuals to "help" their relatives with recommendations, jobs, or contracts, which creates a tension between hiring

and giving contracts to those whom one trusts
(someone known either directly or within the
network, and therefore probably from a specific
ethnic group) and the individual or contractor
with the best qualifications or best proposal.

The Importance of Consensus

Despite the hierarchical nature of Nigerian
society, building consensus among all the
stakeholders up and down the hierarchy and
across departments is of vital importance for the
success of any endeavor. This is probably due in
part to the fact that all Nigerians are proud and,
within their position in the hierarchy, have a
strong belief in their right to be heard. Someone
lower down the hierarchy can block deals or
create tensions. Furthermore, as we have seen,
the mistrust between ethnic groups, and between
ordinary people and their leadership, has fostered
a culture of negotiation and consensus building,
a culture that also applies to the private sector.

Women in Business

It is estimated that women make up about
20 percent of the formal-sector workforce.
Though there are fewer women than men in any
given field, those who do work are respected in
professional circles. Women are doctors, lawyers,
and businesspeople, are engaged at all levels in the
civil service and in government, and are owners
of their own businesses. Women in professional
environments exercise authority over men,
though men continue to be the patriarchs in the

family setting. There are far fewer professional women working in the northern Islamic states, though Muslim women in other states in the south and in Abuja do participate in the informal sector. As there is no state-sponsored child care in Nigeria, someone from the extended family or a hired nanny will look after children. Foreign women will have no more trouble than their male colleagues working in Nigeria.

BUSINESS HOURS

Opening hours for government services and the private sector vary between 7:30 and 8:30 a.m., Monday to Friday. Most large grocery stores open at 9:00 a.m. On Thursdays in Lagos, shops and markets open at 10:00 a.m. after the weekly "sanitation day" designated specifically for businesses. Most offices close at 5:00 p.m., though this, too, can vary—some government offices and most banks close as early 3:00 p.m. On Saturdays, most shops are open. Some businesses close on Fridays in the Muslim north, and very little government business is attended to on Friday afternoons.

Attitudes to Time

In Nigeria, the importance of being on time depends on the circumstances surrounding the event. To urban Nigerians working in the formal sector, time is money and punctuality is generally respected. Foreigners especially are expected to be on time. Even small traders and craftsmen who are accustomed to dealing with foreigners will try to be on time for an appointment, or they will call you to apologize for the delay.

There are several factors that can get in the way of punctuality, however—for instance, the traffic can suddenly block up, and rain can make the roads impassable. Strict adherence to timetables is difficult in a country where personal relations are so important: if a family member or someone higher up in the hierarchy calls, they will get priority over the next appointment on the agenda. Time management is also made difficult because of the limited number of people with the authority to make decisions. Government ministers, for example, are so in demand that keeping to a strict agenda is nearly impossible. Therefore, be prepared to wait. Bring your laptop to help pass the time. Making an issue of the delay will set a bad tone for the meeting and may cost you in terms of goodwill. It is better to simply get on with the business at hand.

Business Dress
It is important to dress formally and conservatively in an office setting and for business meetings in Nigeria. Business suits and ties are appropriate for men, and business skirts that are not too short (just above or anywhere below the knee) for women will

show that you are serious about your work and that you take your Nigerian contacts seriously. In the north and in government circles, many Nigerians will wear national dress, while in the south most people will wear Western-style suits. Because of the heat in Nigeria, it is useful to wear a cotton T-shirt under your shirt or blouse—this will absorb perspiration and leave you looking, if not feeling, fresh.

Business Entertainment

Lunches and dinners are not part of the business culture in Nigeria. If you would like to invite colleagues, clients, or suppliers to dinner, it would be appropriate to do so in the spirit of making good relations rather than trying to accomplish any business dealings. Nigerians do not invite business contacts, or expect to be invited, for a meal. On the other hand, large events such as seminars, networking events, or symposia can include a meal and will be well attended.

Gifts

Exchanging gifts in a business context is not common practice in Nigeria. However, at Christmastime or at the end of Ramadan, or to mark the end of a successful meeting, for instance, you can give important colleagues or business contacts a small gift to show your appreciation: a sample of one of your company's products, for example. It must not be something large enough to be interpreted as a bribe. Something typical from your country, a special food item, or a desk accessory is appropriate. If you receive a gift that you cannot accept, refuse it politely. If the giver insists, accept it graciously and then return it via official lines the next day.

If you organize big meetings, like the seminars mentioned above, or send delegations to Europe or America, it is expected that you will have something (in the nature of a goodie bag) to give all participants: memorabilia with the name and date of the event are most appreciated, such as pens, clocks, or calendars from your company.

MANAGEMENT STYLE

Nigerian culture generally, and therefore the business culture specifically, tends to be hierarchical. Traditionally, age is seen as a sign of wisdom, and respect for your elders is basically a rule. Older people are given the responsibility or privilege of leading a group. The boss expects respect from those below him, and staff expect their boss to act like a boss—he or she should solve problems (even personal ones), make decisions, and give orders. A superior will be addressed by his or her last name (Mr./Mrs. Jones) or by their title (Chief, Sir, Madam, or Boss). Equals may address each other by first name, but it is best to wait until someone invites you to use their first name before doing so.

The Nigerian respect for hierarchy is reflected in the office by a somewhat paternalistic approach to management. A boss is expected to make decisions and to have solutions to problems. He or she may be asked for advice regarding issues in an individual's private life, and expected to resolve conflicts. In the workplace, employees expect to feel "taken care of" or to feel that they belong to the organization's "family." Opportunities for education, training, and travel (especially overseas) are highly regarded incentives.

Foreign employers should give instructions to subordinates politely and respectfully but firmly. They may need to spell out explicitly and unambiguously what is expected. Furthermore, criticizing an employee's work should be done in private and never in public. Important news should be communicated by the boss and moved down appropriate channels.

In terms of discipline, notions of fairness are important in Nigeria. Should a manager have a problem with an employee that requires action, an effective approach is to set up a disciplinary committee to review the case—the decision of the committee will not be seen as the whim of one person or based on personal judgment. Once everyone has had their say, consensus is created and no one will dispute the decision.

Trade Unions

Trade unions are quite powerful in Nigeria. Some of the bigger unions are savvy in their approach: they are well connected and can use the press effectively. When dealing with labor issues it can be useful to have a good human resources professional in place to deal with issues as they arise. From a corporate perspective, a good overall approach is to be open about the company's challenges and to appeal to the union's common interest in finding a solution. A hard-line attitude will be met with a hard-line response. The process requires patience, giving everyone the chance to express their opinions and negotiate a settlement: it is about saving face for all concerned. In the end, creating a relationship based on respect and on the desire to achieve goals together will get things done.

Communication Style

Nigerians are eloquent but tend to be long-winded: the form of delivery is as important as the message itself. This means that interventions in meetings can be quite lengthy. The Anglo-Saxon tendency to get straight to the point with a statement followed by proof of the statement is unusual in Nigeria; Nigerians use proverbs or descriptive language, and arguments are presented in a circuitous manner, beginning with the general idea and slowly moving to the specific.

Another particularity is that subordinates will avoid disagreeing with a superior openly: it is disrespectful and impolite to directly contradict a boss or visiting businessperson. If someone is making a point during a meeting and is trying to negate or critique a point made by a boss, their speech may be even more circuitous than normal. It is therefore important not to assume that everyone has understood what you meant, or has agreed with you. Work that is not being done, or not done according to directives, is probably an indication of the fact that there was disagreement or misunderstanding about what was said. Creative communication strategies may need to be explored—for instance, getting reactions in writing could provide an opportunity for employees to air their concerns without directly contradicting their boss.

Finally, Nigerians in a business context can be emotional communicators. They can be gregarious and enthusiastic, aggressive and loud, or abruptly unforthcoming and taciturn. Foreign businesspeople should remain calm and respectful at all times and try to gain an understanding of the context in which the Nigerian counterpart is acting, such as external pressures to obtain certain outcomes. Keep your goal in mind, be frank and to the point regarding your expectations, and suggest or request options for how to move forward. A positive, solutions-based approach will be greatly appreciated.

Greetings at Work

In a Westernized work environment, people will shake hands. For elders or senior individuals in a Nigerian context, a handshake may be accompanied by a bow or a slight curtsy, eyes averted in respect. When dealing with business partners, handshakes may be held for a long while as initial greetings are made. Handshakes are common before and after meetings. Nigerian men may wait for a female foreign worker to extend her hand first before shaking her hand, and may add a slight bow of respect.

Business cards are very popular in Nigeria, but there is no formal ritual involved in handing them out. However, avoid using your left hand to give or receive business cards and try to pay a moment's attention to the card to show interest in the giver. Your title should be prominent on your card, and it is not seen as conceited or over the top to put university degrees on the card.

CHOOSING YOUR PARTNER

In order to navigate Nigeria's business environment, foreign investors need to have an effective local partner. There are excellent business opportunities, and the government is trying hard to create a climate that is conducive to foreign investment. However, beware of scammers who have the time and energy to create elaborate fake companies with professional-looking Web sites, letterheads, phone contacts, and so on.

Signs of potential fraud are when a Nigerian contact: requests a money transfer or shipment of goods when you have never met face to face; claims to have access to contracts procured from the government; requests advance funds for supplies of local goods; offers an unrealistically attractive business deal that promises quick and large financial returns; claims to be acquainted with highly placed government officials who can facilitate the procurement of huge business contracts; and/or claims to have access to a crude oil allocation from the Nigerian National Petroleum Corporation.

It is imperative that you cross-check any potential partners before setting off for Nigeria. This due diligence process needs to be done by someone whom you trust, who is in Nigeria, and who understands local interests and networks; your chamber of commerce representative, consulate, or embassy are good starting points. Also, the Nigerian Trade Commission in your country and the Nigerian Investment Promotion Council both offer screening services to validate the authenticity of companies.

SETTING UP A MEETING

In Nigeria, important business is conducted during face-to-face meetings. Business meetings should always be set up in advance. There will be a difference between meetings established with the private sector and those with government or parastatal organizations. A meeting should generally be established first by sending a letter of intent, which you or a colleague then follow up on through a telephone call. In government circles, you will need to meet with someone quite senior—decisions are made by very few key and highly positioned individuals—which means that the process of setting up a meeting can take some time. There may be a "gatekeeper" or key person in your industry whom you need to meet first before you can see the decision maker. The Nigerian private sector is far quicker and more efficient in its functioning; setting up meetings in this context will be fairly straightforward.

In your letter of introduction, be sure to state clearly what your intent is and what you hope to achieve from the meeting. In government circles, many departments and even ministries may have a stake in the meeting: the relevant representative from each department will need to be identified and invited. This will entail a careful calibration of ethnic background, networks, and lines of responsibility. Subject experts or specialists may also need to be invited. Everyone will need to be brought on board from the beginning if a successful deal is to be made. It is a good idea to reconfirm your appointment just before the meeting in order to be sure that everyone who should be present will still be able to attend.

AT THE MEETING

On the first meeting with a business contact, be patient and expect to spend time on greetings. Shake hands with everyone present, introduce yourself and your team, and get a clear idea of what area of interest/responsibility each individual has. To rush a greeting is seen as rude and as showing a lack of respect and interest. Your Nigerian host will want to get an idea of who you are and may spend a few moments asking more personal questions, such as about your family. It is polite to reciprocate with similar questions.

In government circles, Nigerians will prefer to arrange one big meeting where everyone can have their say, rather than a series of small meetings. Meetings in both the private and public sectors will most probably be relatively flexible and informal. While only the leader will make a final decision, anyone present can and will participate with questions or comments, though they will take their cue from the top person.

Despite these necessary niceties, time is money in Nigeria and your counterparts will be pressed for time. Meetings will not drag on, and once the introductions are done you will quickly be asked to get down to business. If you are conducting a courtesy visit, it will be important that you listen, try to gain a real understanding for your hosts' concerns and constraints, and show a genuine interest in Nigeria.

Making a Presentation

Don't go to a meeting in either the public or private sector with a lengthy PowerPoint presentation. Rather than make a glitzy presentation that comes across as a hard sell, try to find a shared vision or goal, underpinned with one or two visual aids. In the end, it is all about the relationship and trust, not details and facts.

Negotiations

Nigerians are accomplished negotiators; they are energetic, determined, and well aware of when they have an angle that they can use to their advantage. In government circles, the Nigerian contingent will be large: ideally the decision maker will be present, and it is best to have all concerned parties in the room. For a big deal it may be good to have a sponsor on board, such as a respected statesman or a kingpin in the industry, who could be brought into play should there be a blockage in the negotiations. For private-sector deals the setting will be smaller. Negotiations must always be conducted with respect: do not raise your voice or get emotional. Nigerians will be quite open and straightforward in telling you what is important to them.

CONTRACTS AND FULFILLMENT

Once a contract is established, it will generally be adhered to, but the element of trust and the nurturing of a relationship do not end once the contract is signed. Nigeria can be defined as a relatively litigious society: there is a tendency to run to court if people feel their interests are not met or in order to create an angle or leverage. Sometimes, a court case may be about an internal disagreement between vested interests that do not relate to you or your contracts directly. If litigation does come up, it may be wise to identify a senior Nigerian, someone who is respected in society, to have a look at the issues. If a case does go to court, British common law will apply. A case will first need to be taken to the lower, state court. These courts are seen as less reliable and open to influence. Appeals will go higher up into the federal appeal system and can eventually find their way to the Supreme Court. The federal courts are perceived to provide due process, but the system is slow and costly. For this reason, many cases are settled out of court.

chapter nine

COMMUNICATING

"The city's air is dense with story. The narratives fly at me from all directions. Everyone who walks into the house, or every stranger I engage in conversation has a fascinating yarn to deliver . . . All I have to do is prod gently, and people open up."
Every Day is for the Thief *by Teju Cole*

LANGUAGE

English is the national language in Nigeria; the three other languages used in government are Hausa, Igbo, and Yoruba. English is the language of instruction in all schools; native languages lessons are also given, as Nigerians are multilingual (English is likely to be their second, third, or fourth language). Nigerians educated in private schools and abroad all have a perfect command of the English language and will sound quite British or North American depending on where they studied. Most people, however, will speak their native language at home.

Another language that is commonly used in Nigeria is Pidgin, a mix of English and indigenous languages that serves as a linguistic bridge between classes and ethnic groups. It is used throughout the country and is universally understood, though regional differences exist in terms of words and expressions. It is used in plays and novels, on the radio, and in films. Variations of Pidgin are spoken across West Africa and in the Caribbean, where West African slaves brought the language with them and developed it further.

Just as there are significant differences in British and North American accents, grammar, and expressions, Nigerian English has been affected by the many indigenous languages of the country. Certain words and expressions have a different meaning from what we may expect.

SOME NIGERIAN EXPRESSIONS

"I'm here" means "I'm coming."

"I'm coming now" means "I'll be there in a short while."

"How was your night?" means "Did you sleep well?"

"Sorry" is used often: if you bump your head, people around you will say sorry. It isn't to excuse themselves, but to say "I am sorry that you bumped your head and feel pain."

"Welcome" is much used in the hospitality sense of the word, as in "Welcome to Nigeria." You are welcomed everywhere—at the shop, at the office, or back at your own home (by staff).

"Off the light" means "Turn off the lights."

"The meeting will hold" means "The meeting will be held."

PRONUNCIATION

Accents make some words sound different:
"Fuel" is pronounced "foil."
"Ask" is pronounced "axe."
In Yoruba regions, "s" is pronounced "sh"
(Asa = Asha).
"Cut" is pronounced "court."
"Later" is pronounced "letter."
"Beer" is pronounced "biyah."
Also the intonation is different:
"Represen*ta*tive"
"Vege*ta*bles"

EXAMPLES OF PIDGIN PHRASES

"Se you dey come?" or "You dey come abi?" is
"You are coming, right?"
"Nna, that test hard no be small" is "Man! That
test was hard."
"O" at the end of a sentence puts an emphasis
on a statement—"Sorry o."
A "go-slow" is a traffic jam.
"Wahala" is trouble.
"Wetin dey?" is "What's up?"
"Naija" is the hip word for Nigeria.
"Oyinbo" is a white person.
"How now?" or "How you dey?" is
"How are you?"
"Pikin" is a child.
" I no sabi" is "I don't know."
"Abi?" or "No be so?" is "Isn't it?"

COMMUNICATION STYLES

As we have seen throughout the book, Nigerians are open, warm, and friendly. They are fast thinkers and are quick to offer their opinion or comments. They use beautifully phrased, flowery language peppered with proverbs and sayings. They enjoy talking and chide themselves for being long-winded. To other Africans, Nigerians have the reputation of being louder and more "present" than people of any other nation. They are also known to be more emotionally expressive than many other Africans. They tend to come across as self-assured and outspoken, which can at times be interpreted as arrogant or intimidating to those not accustomed to such directness.

There is a difference between the way that Nigerians speak to older or more senior people and the way they express themselves to their peers or people lower down the hierarchy. To seniors, they will be extremely polite and reserved. They will tend not to disagree and will be less apt to show negative or excessive emotions. To peers or juniors, they may be sharper, more direct, or even blunt, and will express their emotions freely.

Having said that, communication styles do vary across ethnic groups. For example, Nigerians from the Muslim north tend to be more reserved and less direct than southerners, while the Yoruba are said to be the most outgoing and emotional of all Nigerians.

Body Language

With friends, Nigerians are accustomed to having less personal space in public than is customary in many Western countries. When people stand close to you, they are not displaying aggressive behavior but exactly the opposite: it shows a level of comfort with your presence. With friends, Nigerian greetings are warm, including hugs and kisses on the cheeks at informal gatherings. Men may place their hand on another man's shoulder during a handshake. Men will generally wait for a woman to proffer her hand before offering theirs out of respect. Finally, some observant Muslims, particularly in the north, may opt not to shake hands with women for religious reasons.

As we have seen, it is regarded as impolite to use your left hand to give or receive objects, even when passing out business cards. Constant and direct eye contact with a senior person (in age or position) can be seen as being intrusive, cheeky, or even rude. Therefore, if you are being addressed by someone who is not maintaining eye contact, they are not being rude or shifty but are showing you deference and being polite. Nigerians, like many cultures in Africa, will smile or laugh as a response to embarrassment or in acknowledgment of a difficult situation. If you criticize someone or point out a negative aspect of Nigerian life, they are likely to laugh: they are not making light of the point made, but rather saying "Better to laugh than to cry."

To get the attention of a waiter, or someone on the street who is far away, Nigerians call to each other with a kissing or hissing sound. It isn't rude, but as a foreign guest it may be wise not to attempt it in case you use it inappropriately.

In terms of hand signals, a hand outstretched at shoulder level, palm out and fingers spread, is rude—it means something to the effect of "You come from unsure parentage." Particularly in the north, a fist raised at head level with closed fingers facing forward is a sign of greeting—it means "We are one" or "I am not armed" or "Hello friend."

Forms of Address/Proper Acknowledgment
Nigerians tend to be quite formal in their greetings. To say "Hi" is seen as very informal and even impolite—"Good morning" is much better. Inappropriate familiarity is seen as a lack of respect; it is therefore very important to greet people "properly," which means taking the time to really mean "Hello, how are you?" when you say it. Never ask anyone a question (not even "What time is it?") without first greeting them. Always begin with a friendly smile and acknowledge the person you are speaking to with "Good morning" or some such opening. Make eye contact, then you can ask your question. Not to acknowledge someone, no matter how brief the conversation, is seen as rude; you may get a rude, or at best perfunctory, reply. If you are establishing a relationship or friendship with someone, inquiring about a person's health and well-being, and their family, is very important.

As we have seen, Nigerians are age- and hierarchy-conscious. Older people are treated respectfully; they are greeted first, allowed to enter a room first, and so on. In the Yoruba culture it was the custom for people to get down on their knees or even lie prostrate on the ground. While this is no longer seen in the cities, it is still common across the country for men to give a short bow and women, especially young women and girls, to curtsy. Furthermore, it is best always to address Nigerians using their titles. So, instead of using "Mr." or "Mrs.," use "Chief" or "Barrister" or whichever title the individual holds. Unless told otherwise, always address older people by their last names. Using Sir or Madam (accent on the second syllable) is always a safe bet when unsure.

When addressing people further down the hierarchy, however, Nigerians can be less polite. You may hear a Nigerian bark at their driver, or ask their employees to do things in a way that sounds rude. As a foreign guest, however, it is wise to be polite and respectful to everyone, no matter what their status, in order to avoid ruffling feathers unnecessarily.

THE MEDIA
Press
The news media in Nigeria is open and relatively free. There are four main national newspapers and each city has its local papers, including four in Abuja and sixteen in Lagos. Most of these are published in English, though there are papers in local languages as well. Newspapers like *Guardian News*, *Business Day*, and *234 Next* (all also

available online) are serious broadsheets for those wishing to keep their finger on the pulse of what is happening in Nigeria.

Some newspapers are more like public bulletin boards. Alongside legitimate news articles are what amount to advertorials for individuals—people pay for articles, letters, and opinion pieces on themselves or someone else. This is a form of clientelism in which the journalist acts more as a service provider than an independent investigator. Low pay, close relationships between publishers and politicians, and corruption do influence the practice of journalism in the country.

There are several magazines in circulation in Nigeria, catering to special interest audiences. Most of them, however, struggle to survive, with very low subscription rates: *City People* (high society), *Genevieve* (women's issues), *Kick Off* (soccer), and *Newswatch* are examples. For the foreign community, magazines like *Welcome* and *Time Out* (specific to various cities) provide information about what's going on and where to go.

Radio

Many people get their firsthand news from transistor radios. There are stations in every state, and every language has its own station. While most states have one or two stations,  there are between twenty and thirty in Lagos alone. There are two national stations owned by the federal government: Voice of Nigeria and NTA. The most popular station is Wazobia ("*wa*," "*zo*," and "*bia*" all mean "come" in Yoruba, Hausa, and Igbo respectively). Cool FM, the second most popular station—modern, young, and hip—broadcasts in English.

Programming is regulated by the Nigerian Broadcasting Commission, which is directly under the office of the president of Nigeria (and therefore a matter of national security). This means that stations are very careful about taking political positions on the air. They will, for instance, initiate a discussion on a topic and have callers give their opinions but not voice their own. Also, religious programming is not officially allowed under the Commission's guidelines, so many essentially religious programs are labeled "inspirational."

Television

There are five major broadcasters (one state owned and the remainder private), each with several stations, which cover most of Nigeria. Several smaller operators are going out of business because of a government decree that all stations must switch from analog to digital technology by 2014. The stations show programs from around the world as well as a wide selection of popular Nigerian content in many local languages that includes local movies, soaps, news programs, and reality TV shows.

Satellite television is also available. The main company is DSTV out of South Africa. There are also a few specialized satellite companies that offer content for foreign-language speakers. For instance, there is Canal-Plus, which provides several French-language stations, and NileSat for Arabic speakers.

SERVICES
Telephone and Internet Services

Telephone communication in Nigeria is good thanks to a deregulation program implemented a few years ago that led to a highly competitive investment market. Nigeria is currently the fastest growing GSM market in the world, with well over fifty million users. The main providers are MTN (South African), Glo (Nigerian), Etisalat (United Arab Emirates), and Bharti Airtel (Indian). Telephone numbers begin with either 08 or 07, followed by nine digits. The country code for Nigeria is +234.

All GSM operators have roaming agreements with international operators, so an international phone will work in Nigeria, though it will be expensive. It is simpler and cheaper (less than US$2) to buy a SIM card for your cell phone so that you have a Nigerian number (your phone must not be "SIM-locked"). Cell phones are also available in all major cities. Prepaid credit can be purchased from vendors at street corners and in "go-slows."

When making calls in Nigeria, be aware that there are two other telephone systems in Nigeria with shorter phone numbers. One is the landline service (provided by the state company Nigerian Telecommunications Limited, or NITEL), which uses city codes (01 for Lagos and 09 for Abuja). The other, called Code Division Multiple Access or CDMA (provided by Starcomms and Zoom (both Nigerian), and Multilinks (South African)), starts with 07. Both have a total of nine digits as opposed to the cell phone system's eleven; both also have a far smaller market share.

All of the companies above provide Internet services. For private use, they sell a USB dongle for somewhere between US$50 and US$100. Service costs between US$20 and US$200 a month depending on speed and data allowance. Many companies have launched daily Internet plans for those who do not want a monthly cost. The growth rate in the telecoms sector in Nigeria was one of the fastest in the world for the last five years; Internet cafés are popular in all urban centers, and most hotels and many restaurants now have wireless services for their clients.

Cellular telephone and Internet services were made possible in 2003 when NITEL and an African consortium of companies invested in an undersea fiber-optic cable that connects the African continent to Europe. A private cable came online in 2010, further improving service and decreasing costs. A new cable is scheduled to begin offering services in 2011. While they may not be as consistent as in Europe (telephone and Internet services are known to be patchy when it rains, for instance), the explosive development of communication services has been the single biggest boost to the Nigerian economy since the discovery of petroleum in the country.

Postal Services

Nigeria has a modern postal service that has seen great improvements in recent years, particularly since it became a parastatal organization with a degree of independence from the government. Its services, including zip code information, can be found on its Web site or at any one of the post offices in the main cities throughout the country.

Service is still inconsistent, however; home delivery is less predictable than the PO box service at the post office. It is not advisable to send financial or sensitive documents through the mail. For sensitive mail and packages requiring speedy and guaranteed national or international delivery, there are a several local courier services (information is easily available on the Internet) and a few international ones like DHL, UPS, and FedEx. Many provide international freight services as well.

CONCLUSION

Given the importance of its petroleum industry and the growth that has occurred in other economic sectors, Nigeria is potentially a significant leader in Africa and beyond. It attracts many foreigners who come in search of business and career opportunities.

Those who have been here a long time will tell newcomers that things are not always as they seem, and that it takes time and effort to get to know the people and understand their ways. As we have seen, Nigerian society is based on underlying relationships that form complex networks and hierarchies that are opaque to outsiders; it takes time to establish the trust that is the basis for friendship and successful business practice. The strict social norms and expected forms of behavior that are publicly upheld are not always applied in practice, however, because of the famous Nigerian pragmatism and flexibility generated by the need to deal with the difficulties of everyday life. Finally, the extreme diversity of Nigeria's people, in terms of ethnicity and economic standing, makes it difficult to generalize about the nation's "culture."

Nigeria is vast and complex country with varied, rich, and dynamic cultures. The Nigerians themselves, whether through literature, the arts, or personal relationships, exude a pragmatic, positive, and cheerful attitude to life. The country has entered an optimistic period in its development, which makes this the perfect time to visit. We hope that *Culture Smart! Nigeria* will help to deepen and broaden your experience of this fascinating land. Again, welcome!

Further Reading

Achebe, Chinua. *The Trouble with Nigeria* (reissue edition). Enugu: Fourth
Dimension Publishing, 2000.

Adeyemi, Ester. *Contemporary Art in Nigeria and Ghana*. Basel: Friederich
Reinhardt Verlag, 2005.

Falola, Toyin and Matthew M. Heaton. *A History of Nigeria*. New York:
Cambridge University Press, 2008.

Maier, Karl. *This House has Fallen*. London: Penguin Books, 2000.

Smith, Daniel Jordan. *A Culture of Corruption: Everyday Deception and
Popular Discontent in Nigeria*. Princeton: Princeton University Press, 2007.

Williams, Lizzie. *Bradt Guide: Nigeria* (2nd edition). Buckinghamshire: The
Globe Pequot Press, 2008.

To get a sense of the country, there are many novels that are well worth a
read. Here are a few popular titles by well-known Nigerian authors:

Achebe, Chinua. *Things Fall Apart* (1958). New York: Anchor Books, 1994.

Adichie, Chimamanda Ngozi. *Purple Hibiscus*. Chapel Hill: Algonquin
Books, 2003.

———. *Half of a Yellow Sun*. New York: Anchor Books, 2007.

———. *The Thing around your Neck*. New York: Anchor, 2010.

Habila, Helon. *Waiting for an Angel*. London: W. W. Norton & Company,
2004.

Nwaubani, Adaobi Tricia. *I Do Not Come to You by Chance*. New York:
Hyperion, 2009.

Soyinka, Wole. *The Lion and the Jewel*. USA: Oxford University Press, 1966.

———. *Ake: The Years of Childhood* (1st edition, thus.). New York: Vintage,
1989.

Useful Web Sites

www.ldiommosaic.com/wordpress
Blog by Diane Lemieux on various aspects of life in Nigeria.

www.ngex.com/nigeria/
Government Web site with information and news.

culture smart! **nigeria**

Index

Acknowledgments

Special thanks to Mojisola Ayanbadejo-Swartjes, Azu Nwagbogu, Yen Choi, Grant Mowat, Zainab Ashadu, Andrea Ajibade, Danjuma Abdullahi, Efe Wilson, Osagie Aizojie, Mabel Adeosun, Antoine Ganson, Idris Aregbe, Fouad Chalfoun, Bernard Bos, Femi Ogunlende, the ladies of the Niger Women's Club and the ladies of the African Book Group, especially Aduke Gomez, Ijeoma Ejekam, Ayo Inika, Betty Okuboyejo, Ekanem Konu, and Omotayo Adeola.